Lives in Cricket: No 31

GW00600585

Walter Robins
Achievements, Affections and Affronts

Brian Rendell

First published in Great Britain by
Association of Cricket Statisticians and Historians
Cardiff CF11 9XR.
© ACS, 2013

Brian Rendell has asserted his right under the Copyright, Designs
and Patents Act 1988 to be identified as the author of this work

British Library Cataloguing-in-Publication Data.
A catalogue record for this book is available from the British Library.

ISBN: 978 1 908165 35 0
Typeset and printed by The City Press Leeds Ltd

Contents

*At ease, for once. Robbie at The Shrubbery House, Froyle,
where the garden sloped down to the River Wey.*

Introduction

Throughout his life Walter Robins was referred to by a variety of names or nicknames depending upon his relationship to the speaker or writer. Many cricketers are known by two, sometimes three names: Walter Robins had six or seven at least. According to Colin Cowdrey he was 'a small, dynamic man known as Robbie to his cricket associates, Walter to those who were never quite admitted to that magic circle and R.W.V. of Middlesex and England to the public at large'. That list, though, was incomplete because to those who were unsettled by his persistent air of confidence he was 'Cock Robin', and to others who acknowledged his passionate, sometimes headstrong, love of the game but were unable to commit themselves with the same audacity, he was just plain 'Robins' or 'Mr Robins', and sometimes even 'Mr Chairman'.

He was christened Robert Walter Vivian and was the first in the family to be given three forenames. It was customary at one time to give new arrivals in a family the name of a recently deceased relative and the first name Robert probably came from the late brother of Walter's grandmother. Vivian was his father's name and Walter came from an uncle, who during occasional visits to Stafford played cricket alongside Vivian as a slow left-arm bowler. But the new member was welcomed into the Robins family as Walter and it was a variation of that name that became the first of his nicknames after it was noticed that, as a small child, he would often be found singing while playing and it wasn't long before he became known as 'Jolly Wally'. At school he was 'Walter' to his friends, 'Robins' to the other boys, and selection for 'The Rest' against 'Lord's Schools' at Lord's in 1924 saw the first appearance on a scorecard of 'R.W.V.Robins'. For his debut for Middlesex in 1925 he was recorded in the style for all amateur cricketers appearing in county cricket at that time as 'Mr R.W.V.Robins.' Arriving at Cambridge University that autumn he embraced all aspects of undergraduate life, sporting and social, with such uninhibited zeal and verve that his universal popularity soon earned him the nickname of 'Robbie'. But to close family and friends he was always 'Walter', although in her first letters to him, his future wife Kathleen Knight observed the correct etiquette and addressed them to 'Robert'.

One of his earliest and closest friends was Ian Peebles of Middlesex and England and he would have been the ideal person to have written a biography as he knew all aspects of his friend's intractable and impatient personality, and admired him because he was 'fiery and determined and had the courage to be outspoken on all occasions'. His younger son, Richard, believes that his father 'threw everything into any game he played and took on the contest at the charge — not specifically because he wanted to entertain, but because that was the only way he knew how to play — the cricket world saw him as a cavalier character but nobody loathed losing more than he did!' It was as a footballer that his lion-hearted and tenacious character could be fully exploited as he took the ball at high speed along the touchline at outside-right looking to create or score goals for Cambridge University and later for the famous amateur club Corinthians who, when at their best, could compete with the leading professional clubs of the day.

With maturity came responsibility and authority within the world of cricket, both of which he welcomed with his customary enthusiasm. Christopher Martin-Jenkins thought him 'an administrator as lively and enterprising as he had been a player'. To him it was essential that the game must be played with intelligence, technical skill and vision. He always stuck to the basic principle that there was a right way and a wrong way to play the game and when he was right his overwhelming self-belief overcame those who may have had doubts and success would follow. But when he was wrong that same self-belief led him to ignore good counsel and arguments followed. His lifelong habit of telling it exactly as he saw it earned him some antagonists as he did not suffer those he viewed as fools gladly and, as his wife Kathleen recalled:

> He had a very quick temper, which he never controlled because, I think, he considered it a good trait. I also suspect that he held the theory that if anything happened to annoy him, it was useless just to remonstrate with those responsible, but to make an absolutely terrific hullabaloo then ten-to-one it would not occur again. I expect this made many enemies, but they only remained enemies for a short while as it was all froth and bubble, and he never remembered his violent outbursts.

His elder son, Charles, agreed: 'quick fire anger (with speed to forgive) made him never that easy to live with.' Whatever arguments might have ensued, it should never be forgotten that, according to Peebles, 'he had a glorious sense of humour' and that when necessary he 'brought an impish, urchin-like, but timely levity which would flash out to relieve the heated or gloomy moment.' That humour was enjoyed by many and during a visit to Australia, John Bradman, the son of Sir Don, told Richard Robins that 'your father was the funniest and most irreverent man I've ever met'.

Both sons, Charles and Richard, were given three forenames like their father and uncle before them. First there was Robert Victor Charles (R.V.C.) Robins, then George Richard Vernon (G.R.V.) Robins. Within the family over the years it became easier to refer to Walter Robins as 'R.W.V.' and in all my conversations and on-line communications with Charles and Richard it has been with those initials by which we identified their father when exchanging questions and answers. There no evidence to support the suggestion by Cowdrey that he was known as 'R.W.V. of Middlesex and England' to the public at large, and his close friendship with Ian Peebles for over forty years has already contradicted the other assertion that he was only 'Walter to those who were never quite admitted to that magic circle [of his cricket associates].' Charles Robins suggested to me during the writing of this biography that 'Somewhere between Richard and I you should get the right flavour!' But after I was allowed access to the private memoir of their mother, another, unique, view of Walter Robins, the husband and father, as well as the sportsman, was revealed. I had already gathered a collection of conflicting views from a variety of cricket historians, players, commentators and administrators and had still not yet formed a clear picture in my own mind of the true character of the man whose life I wanted to present.

After publication of 'Gubby Under Pressure' in 2009, I had become uncomfortable with the picture I had presented, based on the contents of the letters written by Allen, of Walter Robins as an irresponsible member of the MCC team in Australia in 1936/37, who had failed to give the support needed by Allen from his vice-captain during Allen's stressful struggle with the pressures of captaincy. Looking more closely at the day-to-day history of the tour, I realised that such an assessment was unfair. Walter Robins had played a huge role in ensuring the successful continuation of the tour during Allen's frequent absences and, rather than receiving criticism from Allen, he was entitled to an enormous debt of gratitude. Wishing to put the record straight, a biography seemed the obvious route, particularly as other stories about him had appeared in various books and autobiographies which, in several cases, did not always appear to do justice to someone who had obviously been a charismatic character and outstanding cricketer before and after the war. It would be a challenge as there were no personal diaries, no more than a handful of letters, and a brief but concise manager's report to MCC after the 1959/60 tour to the West Indies. Fortunately, both sons, Charles and Richard, were willing to co-operate with my efforts and their memories of many personal events during their father's life, some dramatic, some comic, that had never been aired before, together with the private family memoir of their mother which included important extracts from the correspondence between Walter and Don Bradman, another close friendship that had lasted over thirty years, helped me to put together what I hope is a true picture of the sportsman and the man.

Of the many identities given to Walter Robins I now believe there is one which encapsulates the essence of his personality. From the moment he arrived at Cambridge University and during the four years he was in residence he threw himself whole-heartedly into the pursuit of as many sports as time allowed, to the delight of every group of undergraduates who welcomed his participation. The sheer fun and joy of taking part, of playing and winning — although losing was acceptable if everyone had played the game to the best of their ability — made every day worthwhile. That is when he became known affectionately to all as 'Robbie', and despite all the adult responsibilities and duties which followed, which he accepted without question, at heart he never stopped being that young man at university.

Chapter One

Early Years in Staffordshire

Stafford had been a small market town, just like many others in the Midlands, until the nineteenth century when William Hopton introduced machines for the mass production of shoes and built long rows of terraced houses for his factory workers. That enterprise eventually failed but by the start of the twentieth century it had been replaced by the development of factories in Stafford serving the railway industry and Stafford was a thriving, although predominantly working-class, town once more, augmented by a hard core of lower-middle-class families like the Robins.

The 1901 Census records that Harry Robins, a 45-year-old railway clerk, was the 'head' of the household at 52 Lichfield Street in Stafford. He and his wife Leticia, aged 40, had three sons and three daughters living with them. The eldest son was Vivian (20), a postal clerk, and his two younger brothers were Veral (19), a railway clerk, and Vernon (15). The three girls were Vera (17), Gwen (12) and Valeria (7).

By 1901, Vivian was already a cricket-playing member of the Stafford Cricket Club. The club played at The Hough which they leased from the King Edward VI Grammar School. Tennis courts were available to full members paying an annual subscription of one guinea and those courts were to be the scene of an unfortunate incident when a quick-fire angry response to criticism could have seen the end of Vivian's cricket career at Stafford before it had hardly begun. At a committee meeting on 21 January 1902 it was recorded that

> A complaint was made by Mr Shaw respecting the conduct of Mr V.H.Robins during the cricket season. Mr Shaw said he had occasion to remonstrate with Mr Robins in playing lawn tennis, Mr Robins not being a guinea subscriber, and alleged that Mr Robins used bad language towards him. Having heard the complaint, it was resolved, on the motion of Mr J.Hall, seconded by Mr R.H.Webb, that a letter should be written to Mr Robins informing him that unless he apologised to Mr Shaw by letter he would be expelled from the club.

At the Annual General Meeting of the club at the Alexandra Hotel in Stafford a week later the matter had been resolved, whether by retraction of the original complaint or by written apology is not recorded. What was recorded was the election of Mr Shaw to the position of treasurer and the election of Vivian to the committee where future minutes would confirm that they both met at regular intervals without rancour. In the summer of 1904 Vivian won the batting prize of a new bat, value twenty-one shillings, for coming top of the batting averages. His father, Harry Robins, was elected member of the club that year and at the next A.G.M. was voted on to the committee, on which he served continuously from 1905 to 1911. Veral Robins was also elected a member in 1904 and Vernon in 1905.

Sometime in the summer of 1904, the young Mabel Scott entered the life of Vivian Robins. Daughter of a wealthy mining engineer, John Scott, living at Kidderminster in Worcestershire, she had come to stay in Stafford with a friend whose father was the Lord Lieutenant of the county. Mabel was glad to be escaping the restrictions of a home where her father imposed strict rules of behaviour on his three daughters. At Stafford discipline was more relaxed and Mabel and Miss Williamson were even allowed to go horse-riding together without a chaperone. On one of their rides they encountered Vivian Robbins on his bicycle and he was able to offer some assistance to the riders. Further meetings took place between Mabel and Vivian alone and towards the end of her visit a clandestine marriage took place. Mabel returned home where she intended to wait until she heard from Vivian that he had made arrangements for her to join him and that their marriage could be announced. But her secret was revealed and after an argument with her father Mabel went back to Stafford earlier than she and Vivian had planned but was immediately welcomed into the home of the Robins family.

Modest beginnings. Robbie was born in this street in Stafford in June 1906. Photograph taken in February 2013.

Vivian continued to make progress with his career with the Post Office and soon he and Mabel moved into their new home at 15 Corporation Street. In 1905 they celebrated the birth of their first child Eleanor Letitia, followed a year later, on 3 June 1906, by Robert Walter Vivian, and a year after that by William Vernon Harry. Fatherhood seems to have agreed with Vivian as he was elected captain of the club's Wednesday first eleven in 1905, won the first-eleven fielding prize in 1906 and in 1907 'scored more runs than any other member of the club in first-eleven matches' and obtained a fair number of wickets.

Grammar School boy. Robbie (left) with sister Letitia and brother Vernon.

The census for 1911 shows that Vivian had now progressed to the position of sorting clerk and telegraphist with the Post Office. Not long after the census was taken, all three children, Walter, Vernon and Eleanor, were spending most of the day at Lichfield Street in the care of their Auntie Vera, as Vivian and Mabel had moved the family into a larger house, Green End, in the High Street, where Mabel was taking student lodgers while Vivian was working longer hours.

The influence of the Robins family within the Stafford Cricket Club had grown with the passing years; in 1911 Vernon was voted general secretary and Vivian the match secretary. In 1912 Veral became the vice-captain of the Saturday second eleven and Vivian returned to the Wednesday firsts as vice-captain. From 1902 to 1912 Stafford Cricket Club first eleven played 341 matches, winning 43% and losing 29%. They reached the semi-final of the North Staffordshire Cup in 1904 and the final in 1906, played at the County Ground in Stoke. The club will celebrate its 150th anniversary in 2014 and today boasts four Saturday elevens, one Sunday side, and four junior teams.

Vivian's personal figures for the first eleven for all the seasons from 1903 to 1912 — records and averages for the 1913 and 1914 seasons have not survived — showed that he played in 199 matches and scored 4,069 runs at an average of 25.18. He also took 370 wickets at an average of 10.00. He played occasionally as an amateur for Staffordshire in the Minor Counties Championship alongside the great Sydney Barnes, and on one memorable occasion against Cheshire carried his bat against the hostile bowling of Walter Brearley. Vernon Robins played in 83 matches for the Stafford first eleven and scored 931 runs at an average of 13.50; Veral Robins played in 25 matches for the first eleven.

Going to watch their father and both uncles playing at The Hough, where the cricket ground was a short walking distance from their grandparents' home, would soon be an introduction to the world of cricket for young Walter and his brother. Another important influence at the time adding even more to Walter's growing interest in the game was the discovery of *Wisden Cricketers' Almanack.* Writing in *The Cricketer* Winter Annual in 1967 he remembered spending time in his grandfather's house in Lichfield Street one weekend in 1912. While Harry Robins dozed in his armchair Walter's attention was caught by a small, pale yellow book on the bookshelves. He was fascinated by its contents and, careful not to disturb the sleeping owner, 'borrowed' the book and took it home, where he spent every spare minute reading it from cover to cover. Returning the book the following weekend he discovered all the other *Wisdens* in Harry's collection and, one by one, he 'borrowed' them all, eventually with permission once his grandparent realised what was happening. That early introduction to the importance of the preservation of cricket history stayed with him for the rest of his life and in due course he inherited Harry's complete set of *Wisden* almanacks, when halfway through his second reading of the collection, in 1932.

The outbreak of the Great War in 1914 changed everything for everyone, including the Robins family. The Army immediately recognised the value of the skills of a telegraph technician and Vivian was soon in uniform. He was not sent to the fields of Flanders but to East Africa where news of the movements of German colonial forces needed to be communicated quickly and accurately by telegraph so that an appropriate response could be organised.

The young Walter had begun to attend King Edward VI Grammar School, where the headmaster was Ernest Ormsby Powell, a Hampshire county cricketer in the 1880s with a first-class century to his name, 140 against Somerset. Powell had been a member of Stafford Cricket Club since Vivian's earliest days in 1902, serving on the committee and chairing meetings as well as playing an occasional match and ensuring that the club's lease on the ground was renewed every five years. He immediately recognised the sporting talents of Walter who appeared to have inherited his father's football skills as well as his cricket ability. Vivian had played every winter for Stafford Rangers and had trials for West Bromwich Albion and Aston Villa as a young man. With Powell's encouragement, young Walter played regularly for the school cricket first eleven for two summers and for the football first eleven for one winter. He also loved singing and was a member of both church and school choirs.

In 1915 Mabel left Stafford and went to London where her brother-in-law had arranged for her to work in a Government department. She took a flat in one of the less aristocratic corners of Mayfair, where Walter and Vernon could join her during their school holidays before returning as boarders to their grammar school in Stafford.

Keen young lads. The King Edward VI school side of 1920
with Walter seated fourth from left.

Chapter Two
Highgate and East Molesey

At the end of the war Vivian, now promoted to Warrant Officer, decided to continue his career with the Army and in 1921, after being promoted to Warrant Officer Class I and posted permanently to London, moved the family down with him. Immediately after they had taken up residence in Pimlico, Mabel Robins went to see the headmaster at Highgate School and, despite being unable to meet the full cost of the appropriate boarding-school fees, convinced him that her son Walter was exactly the right class of pupil the school needed at that time. Dr John Johnston believed that the reputation of a public school benefited from the sporting achievements of its pupils and he was the driving force in the battle for the growth of the school. When it came to sports, 'his enthusiasm on the field knew no bounds; disaster touched him on the raw, triumph produced in him paroxysms of delight.'

It appeared that, thanks to his mother's determination, Walter was about to enter the perfect environment for his future development. Eager to raise the standard of cricket played at Highgate, Dr Johnston had, as early as 1912, engaged the services of Albert Knight as coach. Knight had appeared in three Tests for England in Australia during the tour of

The Robins family lived in this house at 22 Cambridge Street, Pimlico in the early 1920s, thus giving Robbie a residential qualification for Middlesex. Photograph taken in February 2013.

1903/04 under the captaincy of Plum Warner, and had played county cricket for Leicestershire from 1895 to 1912. In 1906 he had published his book *The Complete Cricketer* which C.B.Fry declared was the best book on cricket he had ever read. Knight's studious approach to the skills of batting, bowling and fielding found an attentive audience among the schoolboys in his charge and would provide the foundation for the more creative talents of Walter Robins.

Fourteen-year-old Walter entered Highgate School in April 1921 but was considered not yet ready for the school's cricket first eleven. Nevertheless, he showed his potential in matches for School House against the other houses, although the school magazine ominously warned that 'he should prove a good bowler and a useful bat, if he will avoid the pitfalls of youth.' It seems that at school he was medium-fast bowler, and did not 'blossom forth' as a leg-break bowler until later, at university.

But when winter arrived and the soccer season began, restrictions of age and size were cast aside and he was welcomed into the school's football first eleven. The school magazine reported that he was 'small but full of go. Plays hard all the time.' The following season, 1922/23, he was appointed captain and described as 'a clever dribbler and untiring worker who never gives up.' In 1923/24, now 17, the magazine heaped even more praise on his soccer skills: 'Robins has proved himself the best captain of recent years and much of the credit for a successful record is due to the keen, energetic and able way in which he discharge the duties of his responsible office.' In the 1924/25 season, his final winter before going up to Cambridge University, he scored 25 of the school's 69 goals in their 21 matches.

RWV
Robins.

Cartoon of Robbie from the Highgate School magazine of 1925.

However, it was on the cricket field that Walter's greatest schoolboy triumphs would be celebrated. In 49 matches for Highgate in the four seasons from 1922 to 1925 he scored 2,459 runs at an average of 53.32 and took 177 wickets at 15.21 apiece. Against Aldenham School in 1924 he scored 206 and took seven for 54. Another outstanding performance in that same year was at Canterbury against King's School on 8 July, when he opened the batting as usual and scored 67, and followed it up by taking nine wickets as the hosts were skittled out for 36. On returning to Highgate he was summoned to the Headmaster's study where Dr Johnston told him that it was a great day in the annals of the school. Walter modestly replied that it was one of those lucky occasions as he was dropped a couple of times early on and the opponents were a very young side. 'I don't know what you're talking about, Robins,' the Headmaster replied, 'but

Douglas Lowe has just won the Olympic 800 metres final in Paris!'

While Walter was attending Highgate School, his uncle Vernon had accepted the position of Secretary of the National Union of Manufacturers whose London offices were in Holborn, and moved with his wife Eva to Kingston upon Thames. With no children of their own they took great interest in the progress of their nephews Walter and Vernon. From a cricketing point of view Uncle Vernon's arrival in the south brought the Robins family even closer together because he immediately joined the East Molesey Cricket Club at Hampton, next to the River Thames, which was near his new home, and soon persuaded Vivian and Mabel to move nearer the club so that Vivian could do the same.

The Highgate School side of 1924, the first year of Robbie's captaincy. Standing (l to r): R.C.Clarke, K.B.Moore, C.R.Orr, J.W.Luck (wk), C.O.M.Morris, C.W.Fry. Seated: R.L.Stuart, G.N.Paxton, R.W.V.Robins (capt), J.A.Carter, G.D.Hodson.

During the summer school holidays, Walter and his brother Vernon, the latter now at University College School, enjoyed being taken to East Molesey to watch the matches at the weekend and particularly during the Club's cricket week at the end of July. After his impressive successes at Highgate in 1924, Walter had hopes of being given a place in the East Molesey eleven that year but most of the adults were unwilling to risk the inclusion of a schoolboy. Uncle Vernon did not agree and had a word with his friend Alfred Forsdike, the captain of Surbiton Cricket Club, who deliberately brought his team two players short for their annual fixture. It was agreed that both Walter and Vernon could be co-opted into the visitors' eleven and after winning the toss Forsdike sent his new recruits in to open the innings. Facing their father's bowling, the two boys set about hitting him, and the rest of the East Molesey attack, all over the field. Walter made 102 and Vernon 72. Walter was welcomed into the East Molesey team immediately afterwards and went on to play eight times for them that summer, although he was overshadowed by his father who headed both batting and bowling averages.

Uncle Vernon was less successful than his brother, but his enthusiasm won many admirers at the club and three years later he was voted captain, a position he would hold for nearly twenty years. His name in the scorebook was always prefaced by his military title, Lieutenant-Colonel, a commission he had earned while serving in the Great War. His most famous achievement for the club, however, was not actually on the field of play but would be revealed twelve years later.

It came as no surprise that Walter was chosen to play at Lord's in 1924 for The Rest against Lord's Schools. The Lord's Schools team was selected from the boys who had appeared in one of the four Public School matches played during the previous two weeks at Lord's. The selection of The Rest eleven was based on recommendations and reports received from the remaining public schools throughout England and Wales. Brimming with confidence, Walter opened the batting and scored 97 runs. This fine innings was later described by R.L.Hodgson, writing as a 'Country Vicar' in *The Cricketer.*

> A short, squarely-built boy was hitting the bowling all over the field and running between wickets like a rabbit. The nearer he got to three figures the more freely he played. It was a delightful innings [and] he fully deserved a century, if only for the way in which he never slowed down.

Walter was brought back down to earth in his second innings when he was bowled for nought but The Rest ran out winners by five wickets. In the follow-up game at Lord's two days later, playing for the Public Schools eleven against The Army he was again soon out for only a single and then ten in the second innings. This lack of success was the wake-up call he needed and when asked to play for a Public Schools side against Battersea he made an heroic 30 out of an innings total of 96. Playing for Middlesex Club and Ground against Hornsey he had completely recovered his previous form with 89 out of 183 and before returning to school for the autumn term, he top-scored with 50 out of 155 for the Middlesex Young Amateurs against the Essex Young Amateurs on the County Ground at Leyton.

In 1925 Walter was selected again to play at Lord's for The Rest against Lord's Schools at the beginning of August, followed by another appearance in the Public Schools eleven against The Army. His 74 runs from three innings were less than expected and only two wickets from 23 overs at a cost of 84 runs even more disappointing. It was as a batsman that Walter was then asked to join the Middlesex team at Worcester to make his debut in a County Championship match. Perhaps he was a little overawed at finding himself in the same eleven as Harry Lee, Nigel Haig, Patsy Hendren,

'Young' Jack Hearne and Jack Durston, under the captaincy of Frank Mann, because going in at 54 for two he was almost immediately bowled by Fred Root for nought. He was one of Root's six victims in the innings, which may have given him some consolation, and he didn't have to bat again in a low-scoring match won by Middlesex in two days.

Moving on to Birmingham, he took the opportunity to show something of his fighting qualities and earn the respect of his professional and amateur team-mates. In reply to Warwickshire's 408, Middlesex had collapsed to 95 for six when Walter strode out to the middle. Three more wickets soon fell and he was joined by last man, Jack Durston, at 112 for nine. They proceeded to add 73 for the last wicket with Walter's 39 the top score of the innings. Bad weather intervened and Middlesex managed to draw the match.

In his last appearance for Middlesex that summer, against Somerset at Taunton, he was to be involved in an even more dramatic situation. Going in at 192 for six in the first innings he was last out when the total had reached 244 after scoring 36 of the last 52 runs. But when the third day arrived with Middlesex needing 172 runs to win he went to the wicket with the score at 163 for seven. A vital partnership with Durston of five runs took Middlesex to within four runs of victory. He was desperately disappointed at not being able to steer Middlesex home when he was caught off the bowling of Bridges, but Middlesex managed to win with their one remaining wicket intact and Walter could join in the team celebrations.

A place in Queens' College at Cambridge University now awaited him but there was still the problem of finance. At that time there were no student grants or loans, but once again, Dr Johnston came to the rescue. He searched the school financial records and noted that not all of the money raised from voluntary subscriptions to erect a memorial in honour of those ex-pupils and teachers who had fallen during the Great War, had been used. He created a 'War Memorial Scholarship' of £80 per year and promptly awarded it to a grateful Walter Robins.

Chapter Three
Cambridge and Aubrey Faulkner

Walter arrived at Cambridge in time for the freshmen soccer trial matches in October 1925. Despite stiff competition for places with the arrival of a number of promising players, Walter was immediately accepted into the team. To the team and its supporters he was soon known as 'Robbie' and as he went on to embrace many aspects of university life with the same enthusiasm, a warm welcome was extended to the popular Robbie wherever he went.

The first match between Oxford and Cambridge Universities was played in 1874 at Kennington Oval. The fixture, played every December just before the end of the Michaelmas Term, soon became the focal point of each season and as many matches as possible were fitted into the eight preceding weeks. Cambridge played a number of traditional fixtures every year against representative services sides, the Amateur Football Association, the Corinthians, the Casuals and the London Caledonians. In an attempt to improve their standard of play there were also games arranged against professional clubs including Arsenal, Chelsea or Tottenham Hotspur.

By the time Robbie arrived there had been 47 Varsity matches with results standing at 21 wins each but Cambridge had not won for the past three seasons and had been badly beaten 4-1 the previous year. He now found himself a member of a football club where everyone was focused on developing a team that could beat Oxford in two months time. Early results were disappointing, although *The Times* was impressed by their accurate and creative passing compared to the more popular long-ball game and reported that they looked likely to be 'the best Cambridge side for years'. This prediction looked accurate when Tottenham Hotspur came to Cambridge with a side that included several first-team players and lost 2-1. Injuries to key players meant only two wins from the last four games before they went to Stamford Bridge to play Oxford in the Varsity match itself and the game ended in a 2-2 draw. Returning to Cambridge after Christmas for the Lent Term there would be no more university matches, but Walter now enjoyed playing for Queens' College against other colleges in matches that were just as fiercely contested.

* * * * * * *

During the 1926 Easter holiday, Robbie was booked into the Aubrey Faulkner indoor cricket school on the recommendation of 'Plum' Warner. The school had just moved from Richmond to new premises at Fulham, closer to central London, and was the brainchild of the great South African allrounder, Aubrey Faulkner. Settling in England after the 1912 Triangular

Tournament he played club cricket at Nottingham up to 1914. He earned a DSO serving in the artillery during the First World War and in 1918 returned to take a position as a schoolmaster at a preparatory school. While at the school he discovered that he had a flair for cricket coaching and in 1925 rented an old garage at Richmond with room for just one matting pitch and a dressing-room. During his playing career, Faulkner had analysed every phase of the game and now he had a simple but comprehensive system of coaching so that he was able to demonstrate the methods that his pupils needed to adopt in a lucid and easily understood manner. Warner was particularly impressed and would write that 'Aubrey Faulkner was, I should imagine, the best of all coaches. And how he worked! No day was too long for him. He gave his all to his pupils.' The school was an instant success and Faulkner was encouraged to move to larger premises in south-west London. He was accompanied by Ian Peebles, his eighteen-year-old 'secretary', assistant and bowling protégé who had yet to make his first-class debut.

When Robbie's first lesson was booked, Faulkner took Peebles aside and advised him that he has been warned that the new student was 'a perky lad and very much "king of the castle" at Highgate'. Details of Robbie's incredible success as a schoolboy cricketer had apparently been accompanied by stories of his self-confidence that were interpreted by envious outsiders as evidence of vanity and conceit. Expecting a young know-it-all unprepared to accept advice, or even acknowledge that there may be errors in his technique, they were pleasantly surprised by his willingness to listen and learn. Peebles recorded that 'We both took an instant liking to him.'

* * * * * * *

There was a shock waiting for Robbie back at Cambridge when he turned up for the freshmen's cricket trials at the start of the 1926 cricket season. Six players who had been regulars in the 1925 season and had played against Oxford that year were back for another year: competition from new arrivals for the remaining places was strong. Failing to impress in his trial match, Robbie heard that, even though he had already played championship cricket, he was not going to be selected for the early games. This was a setback that he was not prepared to accept without making every effort to prove to the Cambridge selection committee that they had made a mistake and he contacted Lord's and offered his services to Middlesex. By a fortunate coincidence, the University's first game was at Fenner's against Middlesex, so he did not even have to travel. Bad weather meant that play was only possible on the second day but at least Robbie had an opportunity to show some of his batting and bowling skills, scoring ten and taking two wickets. While the match was in progress, the Trades Union Congress had called for a general strike and there was a strong rumour that all University matches would be cancelled. Other first-class matches throughout the country were expected to continue, so Robbie returned with the Middlesex team to Lord's for their next game against Essex. The General Strike continued so Robbie remained in London and played for Middlesex against Somerset when he did not bowl but contributed 17 to a stand of 75 with Patsy Hendren while the veteran completed another century.

The strike was called off on 11 May and Robbie went back to Cambridge where he was asked to play in another freshmen's trial. Scoring a bright 64 for the Etceteras against the Perambulators he was called up for the eleven about to play the touring Australian team which included such giants as Collins, Bardsley, MaCartney, Woodfull, Richardson, Ryder, Grimmett and Mailey. At the end of a rain-reduced first day, Cambridge were 134 for five with Robbie not out on one. The next morning he battled on for some time on a wet, awkward wicket before being caught off Ryder for only nine. Even so, as he returned to the pavilion his confidence was given a boost by praise from Charlie Macartney through a well-chewed blade of grass: 'Well plied, bluey.' He was bowled by Grimmett for nought on the final day and the match was drawn, but his captain Tom Enthoven had been so impressed with his enthusiasm and the high quality of his fielding, that Robbie was now certain of a place for the rest of the season. His fielding was forever after outstanding. In one edition of his *Book of Cricket*, Pelham Warner put him as one of 25 fielders in his 'Honour School of Cricket' and, elsewhere in the same volume, refers to the standard of his fielding at cover point, short leg and gully.

Robbie was not called upon to bowl for Cambridge in any of the nine games he played that summer and in eight of those games he only managed to score 140 runs with a highest score of 32. But it was another story when it came to playing in the University match at Lord's. It was played in miserable weather and in a low-scoring game Robbie made 37 in the Cambridge first innings of 178 and when he went to the wicket at 148 for five in their second innings with a lead of only 164 he finished unbeaten with 21 while another vital 43 runs were added for the last five wickets. It was just enough to beat Oxford by 34 runs.

He went on to play three more games for Middlesex that year and ended the season with only 86 runs from his seven innings in a total of six matches. Despite all the encouragement and support he was receiving, there was still a long way to go before he could be certain of a regular place in a county eleven.

But a far greater challenge faced him which could not be avoided, no matter how many runs or goals he scored – his first-year examinations. With so much cricket and football to play, Robbie had found little time for academic work, so the College, reluctant to lose such an outstanding sportsman, suggested that he should request a change to the subjects he was reading for his degree and therefore postpone an examination for another twelve months. This was arranged and Robbie could rejoin his football team-mates in October for another series of matches in preparation for the Varsity match in December.

By comparison with the team of mainly freshmen at the start of the previous season, the 1926 football 'squad' included nine old Blues, including Robbie, and Cambridge went on to win seven of their thirteen games, scoring 41 goals in all. The change in the off-side law had reduced the number of defenders required between the attacker receiving the ball and the goal line from three to two, with the result that professional clubs revised the positioning of their defenders to introduce the new concept of the 'stopper' centre-half. The Universities still regarded their centre-halves as having an attacking role and when Arsenal sent a team to Cambridge with five regular first-team players, it would be a clash of 'old-style' versus 'new-style'. The professionals' system would eventually be adopted by all football teams, but on this occasion the amateurs were unlucky to lose when, with the score at 2-2, Arsenal scored the winner in the 87th minute.

Encouraged by their performance, Cambridge travelled to Stamford Bridge three games later to face Chelsea. The professionals fielded a strong side but were completely out-played and ended up by being barracked by their own supporters. Cambridge opened the scoring from a cross from Robbie and then went 2-0 up soon after. Chelsea pulled one back but went 3-1 down after Robbie scored from long range. A goalkeeping error brought Chelsea back into the game at 3-2 until a series of passing movements ripped open the Chelsea defence, including the 'stopper' centre-half, and Cambridge added two more goals to win 5-2. Cambridge were strong favourites when they returned to Stamford Bridge to face Oxford but it all went sadly wrong for them and they lost by the only goal of the match.

* * * * * * *

There would again be plenty of College football to play during the Lent Term of 1927, after Christmas, but for Robbie there was also the added honour of being invited to play matches for the Corinthians. The Corinthian Football Club was founded in 1882 and there was no fixed rule defining a member's qualifications, but there was an unwritten law confining election to public-school old boys or members of a university. The club had grown in strength and influence, spreading the game around the world with regular tours to South Africa, North America, Brazil and many European countries. And the match at Hampden Park in Glasgow against Queen's Park, arranged on or near New Year's Day every year was played for an unofficial amateur 'championship' of Great Britain. Robbie was asked to make his debut in a home match at the Crystal Palace against Surrey County in which he scored one of the goals in a 3-3 draw, and he was also selected for the Corinthians' last match of the season against the Navy.

Football and cricket were only part of the very busy life at University now being enjoyed by Robbie. He had been featured in the Michaelmas Term edition of *The Dial*, the Queens' College magazine, in an article under the title 'Man of Mark' and it gives a very clear indication of how he had entered wholeheartedly into the sport and social activities of his College. The obvious popularity of Robbie, as he is referred to throughout, had encouraged the author to present the profile very much tongue-in-cheek, knowing that his subject and readers would appreciate the humour. The article had begun by recognising his sporting achievements: 'In 1925 this modest hero, quite unobtrusively, came into residence, and we of Queens that follow athletics with interest and zeal are pleased that it was to Queens that he came. It is not given to many to collect a soccer 'blue' and a cricket 'blue' in their first year.' This was followed by a description of a reclusive student with characteristics every reader would have known were exactly the opposite of the Robbie they had encountered: 'So shy was he that in his first term he was hardly known by sight to most people in College, except perhaps those freshers that lived near him, and to the small select band of constant chapel-goers.' The next amusing exaggeration was, in fact, much closer to a realistic survey of Robbie's many activities: 'So numerous are his many clubs that he can easily do a week without wearing the same tie twice, but while pride of place goes to the Quidnuncs, "Corinth" is well up for second place.' The 'Quidnuncs' was the club for university cricketers, while 'Corinth' was for players of association football and both would obviously have occupied much of Robbie's time. He would have accepted invitations to join other clubs of a less sporting nature but the author could not resist the opportunity to emphasise the passion of this allround sportsman for games of all types with the report that 'Robbie is a good billiards player, and is understood to have a season ticket at a certain local billiard saloon.' And it seems that he had not lost his love of singing, first discovered in church and school choirs in Stafford and developed at Highgate before he arrived at Cambridge, as the article was delighted to report: 'Everyone in College must be familiar with his ringing tenor voice, so often raised in praise of his favourite flower, the tulip.' The tulip in question was a reference to a public house, the Rose and Tulip, an undergraduate haunt that once existed in nearby St Andrew's Court.

Leaving behind student in-jokes and leg-pulling for the Easter break, Robbie headed immediately for the Faulkner Cricket School. He was determined to spend hours working on his batting technique but also on finding and developing a method of bowling that would turn him into a genuine allrounder. He loved fielding and was proud to be considered one of the best but, being the player he was, he disliked being on the outside looking in while others were having a direct impact on the progress of the game by bowling and taking wickets. E.M.Wellings says that, in batting practice at the school, Faulkner tried to reduce Robbie's unusually high backlift by wedging a plank in the netting at an appropriate height, but his habit was so ingrained it had little effect.

The season did not start well. The University team had lost three of its five main bowlers from the previous summer and the new captain Eddie Dawson was hoping that Robbie would step up and take over one of the vacant slots. In the first game at Fenner's against Yorkshire he bowled one over that went for ten runs and during the next four games he bowled 71 overs while taking only three wickets and conceding 245 runs.

However, the situation was about to change dramatically. The University's leading batsman, K.S.Duleepsinhji, who had begun the season with 101 against Yorkshire and an unbeaten 254 against Middlesex, a Fenner's record, in only four hours, was taken ill and would not return that summer. He had been laid low with such a severe case of pneumonia that prayers were offered for his recovery in his college chapel. Cambridge had already lost another promising batsman when Maurice Turnbull had been forced to withdraw from the university for a year due to an injury, so now the batting strength looked as weak as the bowling. The poor quality of the batting seemed to have been confirmed when facing a strong eleven from Nottinghamshire, including Larwood, Cambridge crashed to 21 for three. But then Robbie joined Dawson and together they added 111 for the fourth wicket before Robbie was caught and bowled by Staples for 96. In the second innings he was unbeaten on 54 when the game ended in a draw.

An impressed Dawson decided to withdraw Robbie from the bowling attack to concentrate on his new batting skills and promoted him to second wicket down for the remaining games leading up to the Lord's match in July. Robbie repaid this vote of confidence by scoring 364 runs in his nine innings at an average of 40.44. Against Oxford at Lord's in the centenary Varsity match, despite Robbie's top score of 55, Cambridge struggled to reach 178, but in reply to Oxford's 149, made amends with 349 for nine declared, including a quick 41 from Robbie, batting at four. A target of 379 was beyond Oxford and Cambridge won by 116 runs.

Moving on to join Middlesex for their next seven county matches, six away and one at Lord's, Robbie was not able to repeat any of his previous Cambridge form. Dropped down into the middle order he managed to score only 105 runs in eight innings and to capture two wickets at the cost of 105 runs. There would be time for some more coaching and practice with Ian Peebles at the Faulkner School but his thoughts were soon turned from control of the flight of the cricket ball to possession and control of a football. Appointed captain at Cambridge his new priority was to put together a team finally capable of beating Oxford in December. He may have felt a tinge of jealousy when he bade farewell to his friend Ian Peebles and Cambridge cricket captain Eddie Dawson, who were sailing away on an MCC tour of South Africa, but he would soon be totally immersed in football training and practice.

Robbie's popularity at Cambridge as a result of his important contributions to a successful cricket team, plus the decision to make him captain of the football team, appear to have over-ruled any suggestion of his rustication when he once again was absent from the examination room. In fact, his College now offered him accommodation within the College itself and for his final year at university he shared a staircase with Nigel Wykes, who would join him as a regular member of the Cambridge cricket team that summer, play for Essex, become a teacher at Eton and eventually housemaster for Robbie's sons Charles and Richard.

Robbie was taking control of a squad of players composed almost entirely of freshmen and the first trials demonstrated that ball control was poor and passing inaccurate, so Robbie's first decision was to move himself in to midfield from the wing in order that he could exercise greater influence over the flow of play. Cambridge won 12 of their matches, which was twice as many as they lost, including a repeat of the 1925 victory over Tottenham

Hotspur with Robbie scoring the winning goal. The Varsity Match was played at Stamford Bridge as usual and all seemed lost when Oxford were 3-1 up at half-time. Some inspiring words from Robbie and a second goal from Bryan Valentine immediately brought Cambridge back into the game but the conditions were against them and they were vulnerable to the physically robust game of Oxford who ended winners 6-2.

Before returning to university for the Lent Term in January 1928, Robbie was invited to play again for the Corinthians. Having reached the fourth round of the FA Cup the season before, the ambitious amateur club was looking for young, fast, creative footballers like Robbie and he was soon to become a regular member of the side.

* * * * * * *

Over the Easter holidays of 1928, Robbie and Duleepsinhji, who had now recovered from his illness and was eager to pick up from where he had left off the season before, spent as much time as they could at the Faulkner School. Robbie was delighted to be reunited with Ian Peebles who had just returned from South Africa with much to tell of his Test debut. His joy was short-lived when Peebles told him that he had fallen out with Faulkner but agreed to work during the Easter vacation before leaving. This spurred Robbie on to even greater efforts to develop and improve his bowling technique while he could still take advantage of his friends' advice and encouragement. This intense period would pay huge dividends in the summer to come but was interrupted abruptly by an urgent call from the Corinthians, who were on tour in Denmark, seeking reinforcements to replace injured players for the second leg of the tour in Germany. Robbie arrived in time to play in the game at Hanover won by the tourists 2-1, followed by a goal-less draw at Hamburg against the German champions.

Their boat left Hamburg for England soon after and Robbie was back in Cambridge in time for the start of the cricket season. In the third match against Yorkshire, the reigning champions, Robbie had his first experience of a 'king pair'. But he was not alone struggling against the bowling of Emmott Robinson who took eight for 13 while Cambridge were dismissed for 30 and had only reached 41 for five when the game ended in a draw. Many years later Robbie told Freddie Trueman the story of his second dismissal in that match. When he made his way to the wicket at 19 for three, he passed Wilfred Rhodes fielding at close gully who said: 'You got nought in the first innings didn't you, young man?' Robbie replied: 'Yes, Mr Rhodes, I did.' Rhodes then asked him if he had ever made a pair to which Robbie answered: 'No, no, I haven't,' to which the obliging old Yorkshireman replied: 'Oh, we'll give ye wun to get off the mark,' waving to the fieldsmen in the covers to drop back. The bowler was Maurice Leyland and, after Rhodes had lulled Robbie into feeling that he could just play at the ball for a simple single into the space on the off-side, Rhodes had instructed Leyland to bowl a little higher and wider than usual. As the ball turned quickly it came off the edge of Robbie's bat pushing forward for Rhodes to snap up an easy catch with the comment: 'Bad luck, son, you tried to hit it too hard.' As Robbie turned to walk back to the pavilion

Rhodes added: 'That will teach you not to take notice of old professionals.' It is not known what W.A.Worsley, the Yorkshire captain, made of it all. The incident certainly gave Robbie food for thought: when he played against Yorkshire for Middlesex later that summer, Rhodes couldn't get him out in either innings.

After six matches at Fenner's, during which Robbie had bowled 67.4 overs and taken only five wickets at a cost of 231 runs, he suddenly blossomed into a genuine leg-break and googly bowler when the University embarked on its summer tour. At Northampton he took seven wickets for 87 runs in 32 overs as Cambridge won by an innings. In the next four games he bowled 111 overs and took 16 wickets, but they cost 428 runs and he still needed to work on his line and length to complement his newly developed deceptive flight. At Lord's against an MCC eleven it all came good and he took eight wickets for only 127 runs from 39.4 overs, including six for 61 in the club's second innings, the first time he had taken five or more wickets in a first-class innings. As far as batting was concerned, up to then he had scored 494 runs from 20 innings and had reached 50 only twice. In this game he scored 103, his first three-figure innings in first-class cricket, and added 180 with Ted Killick.

Robbie with K.S.Duleepsinhji at The Oval in 1928. The Cambridge University side in this match included four players who in their time played Test cricket.

Now it was time for Robbie to prove once and for all that he had grown into a genuine allrounder, and the Varsity Match at Lord's was the perfect setting. There was nothing to choose between the teams after each had completed their first innings. Cambridge had started with 291, thanks to another good innings from Killick with 74, a half-century from Duleepsinhji, and 53 from Robbie, and Oxford replied with 287 while Robbie had taken four for 91. On the morning of the third and final day, Robbie went in at 160 for five with Killick and Duleepsinhji both out. Lose another wicket now and Cambridge would be hard pressed to set Oxford a target over 200. This was the kind of challenge that always brought out the best of Robbie. He joined Seabrook and together they added a quick 101 runs with a view to a declaration and time to bowl Oxford out. With his captain gone, Robbie accelerated the run rate and scored 40 of the next 69 runs to reach his century in 105 minutes. Cambridge declared, asking Oxford to score 335 in 215 minutes and with the last pair at the wicket still more than 100 behind, the game looked over. But Benson and Hill-Wood defied the Cambridge bowlers for almost half an hour and with only seven minutes left even survived a sharp chance high up at short leg off Robbie, who had taken another four wickets to finish with match figures of eight for 151 from 52.4 overs, and the match ended in a draw, reported flatly by *Wisden* as 'a most exciting finish'.

For Robbie it was the end of his three years at Cambridge University. In 35 matches he had scored 1,730 runs at an average of 32.64 although, as proof of his ability to rise to the big occasion, his average against Oxford in his three Varsity matches at Lord's rose to 77.00, and he had also taken 49 wickets for 28.08 apiece.

Chapter Four

Test Match Debut

Having left Cambridge without a degree it was perhaps time for Robbie, now 22, to consider his future. A successful 'gap summer' or two, playing regularly for Middlesex, could lead to selection for the Test eleven. As an amateur he would receive match expenses, which at Middlesex could be generous, and by continuing to live at home with the support of his parents, his living costs would be minimal. He hoped to take up a teaching post at a preparatory school for a couple of terms during the winter before returning to the cricket field. He was in no hurry to commit himself to a business career and, with his growing portfolio of sporting achievements, could feel confident that opportunities to enter the world of finance or commerce would present themselves in due course. For now, with no responsibilities or commitments, life was there to be enjoyed and he had every intention of enjoying it to the full. According to Ian Peebles, who would soon become a regular companion in and outside the Middlesex dressing-room, 'The young Robins took life at the charge, and his adventures and romances would occasionally find him, as his enterprise at the wicket, in exposed and embarrassing positions, far from home and beyond human aid.'

One week after the University match, Robbie was back at Lord's playing for the first time in the Gentlemen versus Players annual fixture. It was another awakening for him when he found he had to bowl to batsmen of the calibre of Frank Woolley, Phil Mead, Patsy Hendren, Wally Hammond and Maurice Leyland. He failed to take a wicket in 19 overs while the Players amassed 423 runs. At least, when the Gentlemen followed on 223 behind, he had an opportunity to bring them back into the game going in at No.10. His knock of 25, while helping Percy Chapman add 46, helped give the amateurs a lead of 110. It was not enough and the Players won by nine wickets.

Middlesex were anxious to have Robbie back in the side for the remainder of the season. They had lost one of their other promising young leg-spinners halfway through May when Ian Peebles, who had only just qualified for the county, was offered the prospect of a commercial career in the furniture business, working for Sir Julien Cahn in Nottingham. But Robbie's return to the County Championship found him bowling again to an in-form Hammond who scored 166 out of 539 while Robbie's 35.3 overs cost 126 runs for his two wickets and Middlesex lost by an innings. There was little improvement at Headingley with no wickets at all from 22 overs costing 86 runs. His Middlesex captain, Frank Mann, may have started to doubt the wisdom of encouraging Robbie's ambitions as a leg-spinner until they moved down to Bristol to face Gloucestershire again, where he bowled Hammond for a rare duck while taking a few more wickets. It was the breakthrough he needed and for the rest of August he continued to feature among the leading wicket-takers in the Middlesex attack, including the scalp of Jack Hobbs at Kennington Oval and at Lord's. His batting also improved now that he was going in regularly at fifth wicket down and he passed 1,000 runs for the season against Warwickshire at Lord's.

The 1928/29 football season would see the Corinthians reach the fourth round of the FA Cup for the second time in three years and the club scored over 100 goals. The team was so strong that Robbie was chosen for only seven matches. But when the Easter holidays arrived he was asked to join the Corinthian party for a short tour in France, playing in Paris and Cannes.

* * * * * * *

Abandoning his short-lived teaching career at Stanmore after incurring the displeasure of his employers by appearing at morning school with his gown over his dinner jacket, dress shirt, waistcoat and bow-tie, Robbie had nearly a month to prepare in the nets at Lord's for the start of the 1929 season. He was delighted to find that Ian Peebles was waiting for him there. Although it had been agreed in 1928 that Peebles could occasionally take time off work to leave Nottingham and play first-class cricket in the south, he had found it difficult to serve two masters and, after three appearances for Middlesex in May and June, had decided to concentrate on his new employment for the rest of the summer. It didn't work out and Peebles admitted: 'I still yearned to play first-class cricket.' He handed in his notice, then went home to Scotland where he was persuaded by his parents to go to Oxford University and was accepted at Brasenose College from the following autumn term. A delighted Peebles recalled: 'With this glorious prospect before me I returned to London and had my first full season with Middlesex. It was one of the happiest times of my life.' Robbie would have agreed wholeheartedly with that assessment.

Nigel Haig had taken over as captain of a team with a hard core of four ageing professionals, J.W.Hearne, Patsy Hendren, Jack Durston and Harry Lee, and a bunch of promising young amateurs, most of whom would be unable to play more than a few games in the season. Even Gubby Allen could only make six appearances, although Peebles remembered: 'They were happy days whenever Gubby, Walter and I played together.' Much of the bowling burden fell on the shoulders of Robins and Peebles, Neville Cardus ambiguously commenting, 'Two boy leg spinners in perpetual and young-limbed ardent motion — this was a sight worth going miles to see, especially to see it at Lord's.'

In the first nine matches Robbie took 48 wickets, starting in grand style by taking six Leicestershire first-innings wickets for 29 runs, including a hat-trick. In his book *Mainly Middlesex*, written in a prisoner-of-war camp, Terence Prittie devoted most of a chapter to Robbie's bowling in this match, variously comparing him with the boxer Jimmy Wilde, the Pied Piper of Hamelin, the magician Nevil Maskelyne, and George Gershwin. Robbie surpassed this success with eight Gloucestershire first-innings

*The Middlesex side in 1929, Robbie's first full season of county cricket.
Standing (l to r): R.W.V.Robins, D.L.Russell, W.F.F.Price (wk), J.M.Sims,
I.A.R.Peebles, G.E.Hart, J.H.A.Hulme. Seated: H.W.Lee, J.W.Hearne,
N.E.Haig (capt), E.H.Hendren, F.J.Durston.*

wickets for 69 runs, the best innings analysis of his career, and then match figures of eight for 105 against the eventual champions, Nottinghamshire. His batting was less impressive, with only 27 runs from his first six innings, including another 'king pair'. Dropped down the batting order, Robbie immediately showed that he was no tail-ender by helping Hendren add 103 for the seventh wicket against Sussex and ending unbeaten on 79. Reclaiming his rightful place in the middle order he averaged 45.00 for the next six matches, including 65 against Warwickshire in another century partnership with Hendren. All this caught the eye of the England selectors and Robbie was chosen to play for 'The Rest' in the Test Trial at Lord's starting on 8 June. He failed to take any of the 'England' wickets in their first innings but had Sutcliffe caught by Ames in the second and then dismissed the last four batsmen as they went from 141 for five to 169 all out. It wasn't enough to earn a place for the First Test, as the selectors preferred the spin-bowling partnership of 36-year-old Percy Fender and the England captain 'Farmer' White, aged 38. Robbie returned to the Middlesex team to capture another 20 wickets in the next four matches.

Robbie's Test match cricket potential was reconsidered as the England selectors were now looking for a winning combination after England had only managed to take eleven South African wickets to draw the First Test, and they decided to call up Robbie for the Second Test at Lord's. On the final afternoon, a desperate White declared just after 3 pm leaving South Africa needing 293 runs to win. Losing their first wicket with only nine

This card does not necessarily include the fall of the last wicket.

2d. Lord's ☿ Ground.

MIDDLESEX v. GLOUCESTERSHIRE.

WEDNESDAY & THURSDAY, MAY 15, 16, 1929. (Three-day Match.)

GLOUCESTERSHIRE.

	First Innings.		Second Innings.	
1 Dipper	l b w, b Peebles	24	C. DURSTON. B. ENTHOVEN	111
2 Sinfield	l b w, b Robins	11	C. PRICE b. HAIG	11
3 Hammond	st Price, b Robins	50	C. LEE. B. ENTHOVEN.	134
†4 B. H Lyon	b Robins	26	b. ENTHOVEN.	21
*5 Smith	c Price, b Robins	5	NOT OUT	14
6 Neale	st Price, b Robins	17	NOT OUT	4
7 Stephens	b Robins	2		
8 Harris	b Robins	2		
9 Parker	not out	18		
10 Ford	b Robins	9		
11 Goddard	c Price, b Hearne	7		
	B 15, l-b 4, w , n-b	19	B 15, l-b 5 , w 2, n-b	
	Total	190	Total	321

FALL OF THE WICKETS. 4 WKTS DECLARED.

1-40	2-40	3-120	4-121	5-132	6-142	7-152	8-153	9-177	10-190
1-54	2-270	3-	4-	5	6	7	8	9-	10-

ANALYSIS OF BOWLING.

Name.	1st Innings.						2nd Innings.					
	O.	M.	R.	W.	Wd.	N-b.	O.	M.	R.	W.	Wd.	N-b.
Haig	14	8	12	0	...	...	27	9	64	1	...	...
Durston	5	3	14	0	...	...	19	5	28	0	...	...
Peebles	22	7	51	1	...	...	24	7	65	0	...	...
Robins	32	6	69	8	...	...	14	1	20	0	...	...
Hearne ENTHOVEN	13.2	9	25	1	...	...	15	8	78	3	2	...
HART	...	...	...	...	...	...	2	0	12	0	...	...

MIDDLESEX.

	First Innings.		Second Innings.	
†1 N. Haig	b Parker	14	L. B. W. b. PARKER	6
2 Lee, H. W.	c and b Goddard	24	b. PARKER.	63
3 Hearne, J. W.	c Lyon, b Goddard	2	L.B.W. b. GODDARD.	22
4 Hendren, E	b Parker	0	C. SMITH. b. GODDARD	2
5 H. J. Enthoven	c Lyon, b Goddard	4	b. PARKER.	0
6 R. W. V. Robins	c Stevens, b Goddard	3	b. GODDARD.	
7 G. C. Newman	c Lyon, b Goddard	5	C. SMITH. b. GODDARD	112
8 Hart	not out	5	ST. SMITH. b. PARKER	7
*9 Price	b Parker	6	NOT OUT	18
10 Durston	b Goddard	0	b. GODDARD.	2
11 I. A. R. Peebles	st Smith, b Goddard	2	L.B.W. b. GODDARD	3
	B 4, l-b 4, w , n-b	8	B , l-b , w , n-b	
	Total	70	Total	245

FALL OF THE WICKETS.

1-32	2-40	3-41	4-45	5-51	6-51	7-56	8-65	9-68	10-70
1-	2-	3-	4-	5-	6-	7-	8-	9-	10

ANALYSIS OF BOWLING.

Name.	1st Innings.						2nd Innings.					
	O.	M.	R.	W.	Wd.	N-b.	O.	M.	R.	W.	Wd.	N-b.
Sinfield	6	2	12	0	...	...	...	...	...	...	...	...
Goddard	19.3	9	25	7	...	...	...	...	95	6	...	...
Parker	14	4	25	3	...	...	...	...	101	4	...	...

Umpires—Phillips and Buswell.   Scorers—Burton and Bloodworth.

The figures on the Scoring Board show the Batsmen in.

Play commences at 11.30 each day.

Luncheon at 1.30 p.m.   †Captain   * Wicket-keeper.

Stumps drawn 1st and 2nd days at 6.30, 3rd day at 6.

TEA INTERVAL—There will probably be a Tea Interval at **4.15-4.30** but it will depend on the state game.

GLOUCESTERSHIRE. WON BY 196 runs.

Scorecard showing Robbie's best first-class bowling return, eight for 89 v Glamorgan at Lord's in May 1929.

runs on the board, Christy and Mitchell dug in and looked settled while taking the score past 50. White turned to Robbie for inspiration and his call was answered, as *Wisden* later reported:

Robins going on at the pavilion end broke up the partnership and at once it became apparent the change should have been tried earlier. Making the ball turn a lot and quickly, Robins had all the batsmen in trouble, and when at twenty-five minutes past five South Africa had lost five wickets for 85, victory for England seemed certain.

Then Cameron was hit on the head by a fast rising ball from Larwood and knocked 'senseless' to the ground. After he was carried off play continued but the unhappy incident had dampened everybody's spirits and all real interest vanished. An appeal against bad light was welcomed by everyone and the players left the field at 5.45 anxious to hear that the injured batsman had recovered.

Another elderly spin bowler was called in to the England attack for the next Test and Robbie was cast aside in favour of 41-year-old 'Tich' Freeman, by now rapidly approaching his 150th wicket of the season. Meanwhile, Robbie continued to take bundles of wickets for Middlesex and reached a hundred for the season before the end of July while taking ten wickets in a match for the first time, against Leicestershire at Leicester, and sharing all ten second-innings wickets with Peebles, as well as contributing 89 to a fourth wicket partnership of 160 with Hendren.

The next Middlesex game was at Worcester against the county which had finished last in the Championship for the three previous seasons. Once again Worcestershire languished at the bottom of the table and Robbie spurned the opportunity to take some easy wickets as well as building his batting average, by asking Haig if he would mind if he skipped the match and joined the Robins family for the East Molesey Cricket Week. Permission granted, he played in four of the eight matches alongside his father and Uncle Vernon. Father and son, bowling in tandem — and no doubt in competition with one another — took most of the opposition wickets that fell, 22 out of 33, and East Molesey won three of the four matches, with the other unfinished because of rain.

One week later, Robbie and Peebles shared all ten wickets in an innings again, this time against Lancashire at Old Trafford. Peebles was now getting into his stride and his own haul of wickets during August exceeded Robbie's by 46 to 40. Meanwhile, Robbie had entered a purple patch with his batting in the last four county games of the season and scored 351 runs for an average of 70.00, including his maiden championship century, 105 at Taunton against Somerset, while enjoying yet another three-figure partnership with Hendren. But there was even more success to come. Nottinghamshire had finally broken the Lancashire and Yorkshire grip on the Championship that had lasted for seven consecutive seasons, and as new champions, they now faced a challenge from a strong Rest of England eleven at The Oval. Robbie was selected and demonstrated that he was among the top half-dozen allrounders in the country. After taking three lower-order victims in Nottinghamshire's first innings, he played a vital role in a century seventh-wicket partnership with Maurice Leyland while scoring 45 in The Rest's second innings and then destroyed Nottinghamshire's second innings with six for 89 to help deny the champion county's victory by eight runs. Robbie finished the season with 1,134 runs at an average of 26.37 and 162 wickets at an average of 21.53. Peebles summed up his friend's bowling talents:

> Walter Robins at this time was the best English leg-tweaker I ever saw. He bowled at around medium pace with a fine, long, swinging action, and spun the ball more than anyone else in the game outside Australia. His googly was hard to read and came off the pitch with the same venom as the leg-break. He made no great pretensions to flight and was occasionally erratic, but his pace and spin discounted this.

Robbie was nominated as one of the five 'Cricketers of the Year' in the *Wisden* for 1930. The almanack approved of his 'hard hitting' and his cover fielding but there was some reservation about his bowling potential:

> As a googly bowler, he still has something to learn, his fault being that he tries to bowl too fast, and as his trajectory is consequently much lower than that of, say, Freeman, his flight is rarely deceptive. For his success he relies on his very powerful finger-spin which enable him to make the ball turn quickly and at a sharp angle. On his day, he is likely to run through any side but much of his good work is spoiled by erratic length. As a batsman he is a fine driver, hitting the ball very hard on either side.

Peebles disagreed with the *Wisden* assessment: 'He was then unfortunately prevailed upon by some pundits to flight the ball and, though always a rare good tweaker, never fulfilled his glorious potential.'

* * * * * * *

Less than four weeks after the end of the cricket season, Robbie was playing football for the Corinthians. But as much as he was enjoying his football, the 23-year-old Robbie realised that he could not expect his parents to continue to feed, clothe and provide a home for him indefinitely, as willing as they may have been to do so. That autumn he had also started to 'step out' regularly with Kathleen Knight, the daughter of a senior Lloyd's underwriter, and grand-daughter of Sir Henry Knight, Lord Mayor of London in 1882/83. They had met at a golf course in East Molesey when Kathleen had been asked by a girlfriend to make up a foursome with Robbie and his friend. Kathleen wrote in her memoir: 'Walter was far too full of himself and I was not at all attracted, but he invited us out to dinner in London the following week and of course I accepted!' Kathleen was very attractive but a reserved and serious young lady taking a drama course at the Royal Academy of Music and not easily impressed. Nevertheless, Robbie was determined to win her over and invited her as often as he could to go dining and dancing with him at the Berkeley Hotel, a popular place with his friends, and Kathleen enjoyed her introduction to the social side of London at what was known as a 'debs' dive'.

So Robbie was delighted when his growing reputation as a successful allround sportsman had attracted the attention of the management of the national newspaper, the *Daily Mirror,* who offered him a position in the advertising department at a starting salary of £200 per year. But then there arrived what might be an even more intriguing offer. Mabel Robins took a telephone call from Sir Julien Cahn who asked her to pass on the message that he had a proposition for him and would like to hear from him as soon as possible. Robbie was reluctant at first to return the call. He did not relish the idea of becoming another of Sir Julien's cricket mercenaries who were expected to play for his cricket sides as a condition of their employment with the Nottingham Furniture Company: in particular he remembered the reaction of Ian Peebles, now at Oxford University, to life in Nottingham away from regular first-class cricket. His mother persuaded him that nothing would be lost by just attending a meeting to hear what was being offered by the millionaire businessman, and so he called back and an appointment was arranged to take place at the Cumberland Hotel near Marble Arch.

Sir Julien explained that he was setting up a new advertising company to market the furniture sold, mostly by means of attractive hire-purchase arrangements, in his many stores throughout the country. The job would be based in Nottingham and offered the prospect of a commercial career and plenty of cricket. Acceptance meant moving to Nottingham, but it was agreed that Robbie could play a few matches for Middlesex if wanted, provided there were no prior claims of business, and that selection to play for the Sir Julien Cahn XI took precedence over any other invitation. For a young player who might have been on the threshold of a promising Test career, this could have been a major sacrifice. But his future employer dispelled any doubts that Robbie may have been feeling about accepting the proposal. He was offering a salary of £400 per year, twice the *Daily Mirror* salary, and a place on the all-expenses-paid cricket tour of South America arranged for early 1930. And until the offices in Nottingham were ready for the staff to occupy, Robbie was free to continue to live in London and play football for the Corinthians. In fact, Sir Julien encouraged his football ambitions and later arranged for him to play for Nottingham Forest in a Second Division match against Barnsley on Christmas Day, 1929. (He played a second and final League game for Forest, against Reading, on Christmas Day the following year.)

When January 1930 arrived it was time for the third round of the FA Cup and the prospects for Corinthians going further in the competition seemed promising as their opponents, Second Division Millwall, who had been quarter-finalists three years earlier, were having an indifferent season. A crowd of 45,000 packed into the Crystal Palace stadium on Saturday, 11 January to see the two teams draw 2-2, including a goal by Robbie. The replay four days later was at The Den, Millwall's ground, which attracted an attendance of 33,000, and was drawn after extra time. The second replay had to be held at a neutral ground and Stamford Bridge was chosen for Monday, 20 January. Many offices in the City of London were emptied that afternoon as excited bankers and brokers made their way to support the amateur team that featured a number of fellow members from the world of finance. *The Times* reported that 'The stands and mounds round

Robbie playing on the left wing for Corinthians.

the ground were packed long before the game was begun, and soon after the start of the match hundreds of the visitors were allowed to sit on the cinder track round the pitch.' The official attendance figure was 58,775.

The professionals had finally got their act together, but it wasn't a pretty sight. *The Times* reported that 'Twice the referee had to speak to members of the Millwall defence for their tactics, and one at least of their players must be considered lucky that he did not have to retire from the game before it ended.' In the previous replay, K.E.Hegan had suffered a fractured tibia after a vicious tackle from Pike, the Millwall right-back, so for this game W.S.Parker was brought in and Robbie switched to outside-left to fight fire with fire. The pair had words early on and then Pike sent Robbie crashing to the ground and the referee was heard to shout at the Millwall defender: 'That's enough of that or I'll send you off!' Robbie couldn't resist the opportunity to remind the official of his leniency in the game before, and shouted up at him: 'Pity you didn't do it last time!' The referee scowled down at him and warned him: 'Any more of that you'll go as well!' Yellow cards all round today, of course.

The match was eventually won by Millwall and the three games of extremely competitive football played over five hours had been watched by over 136,000 spectators. The Corinthians' share of the receipts went a long way towards paying the rent at Crystal Palace for the next two years. Now, though, it was time for Robbie to start preparing for life with Sir Julien Cahn and what some called his 'travelling circus'.

* * * * * * *

Albert Cahn established the Nottingham Furnishing Company in 1885. His son, Julien, was born in 1882 and as a young schoolboy developed a passionate interest in cricket, despite having no natural ability as a player. After starting work in the family business in 1902, he formed a company cricket team and every season up to the summer of 1914 he organised various teams using players poached from other companies as well as his own.

Once the Great War ended in 1918, Julien concentrated on the expansion and development of the business. By 1923 he had achieved his goal and the Nottingham Furnishing Company was the largest credit furniture company in England. It was time to enjoy the fruits of his success and his first thoughts turned to the rebirth of the Julien Cahn XI. He bought a nine-acre site at West Bridgford, adjacent to Loughborough Road, and built his own cricket ground, complete with a superb pavilion comprising dressing rooms, bathrooms, a dining-room, and score box. The pitch and outfield was of the highest standard thanks to his head groundsman, John Gunn, the Nottinghamshire and England player who had recently retired with 535 first-class matches to his name. There was a high, boarded fence enclosing the ground, but spectators were usually allowed to enter free of charge. The ground opened on 4 June 1926 with a match between a Nottinghamshire XI and 'Sixteen Amateurs of the County captained by Mr Cahn'.

The following year Julien Cahn purchased Stanford Hall, a stately Georgian mansion containing 35 bedrooms, standing in a three thousand acre estate. While key structural changes to the mansion were being completed he arranged an eight-week cricket tour of Jamaica for the Julien Cahn XI, the team's first trip overseas.

Stanford Hall, Sir Julien Cahn's home, photographed in 1939: the cricket ground was off to the right. Kathleen Robins reported hospitality here as 'unforgettable'.

35

Following the award of his knighthood in the summer of 1929, Sir Julien began to plan another escape from the British winter. This time South America would be the destination and his side was now composed almost entirely of players engaged in full-time employment in the shops and offices of his vast furnishing business, so retaining their amateur status. Most had retired from first-class cricket, but the others could be released to play for their counties when not needed to play for the company, or their absence from their place of work could be covered. Robbie was the latest addition to this pool of available players, which is why he now found himself on board the *S.S.Avila Star* of the Blue Star Line sailing from Tilbury on 20 February 1930 and looking forward to his first crossing of the Atlantic.

It is fair to say that Robbie's cricket companions were a hodge-podge of ability and experience; many were from public-school backgrounds. Leonard Green, the eldest at 39, had been captain of Lancashire from 1926 to 1928; 'Tich' Richmond, aged 37, had been a regular for Nottinghamshire from 1912 to 1928 and was now manager of the Smart and Brown furniture shop in Nottingham; Frederick Nicholas, aged 36 and ex-wicketkeeper for Essex; F.C.W. 'Lofty' Newman, aged 35, had played for Surrey from 1919 to 1921 and was now a shop supervisor and the private secretary to Sir Julien Cahn for all his cricket affairs; Humphrey Critchley-Salmonson, aged 35, had last played for Somerset in 1928; Charles Flood, aged 33, had never played for any team other than the Julien Cahn eleven; Harry Munt, aged 27, had played once for Middlesex but was now working in wines and spirits in Nottingham; Trevor Arnott, aged 26, was still playing for Glamorgan; Peter Eckersley, aged 25, was the new Lancashire captain; George Heane, aged 25, was playing occasionally for Nottinghamshire; and Cyril Rowland, aged 24, had been a regular player for Wales for the past five years. There was just one player who was younger than Robbie, the 18-year-old Stuart Rhodes, a trainee shop manager and still waiting to make his first-class debut for Nottinghamshire.

The team manager was Henry Swan, aged 50, who had Essex connections and once served on the MCC committee. John Gunn was taken as the team's umpire, and George Shaw, aged 51, dressing-room attendant at Trent Bridge, came as *chef de baggage*. The team's captain, Sir Julien Cahn, was accompanied by his wife, now Lady Phyllis, her personal maid, and his personal barber Louis Dubonikov. Looking around him, Robbie may have wondered what he had signed up for, but it was early days yet and the prospect of plenty of cricket was his priority for the next few weeks.

The tourists reached Buenos Aires on 13 March 1930, and were met by Robin Stuart, President of the Argentine Cricket Association and then escorted to the Plaza Hotel. Net practice in the afternoon was followed by an informal reception at the English Club and an opportunity for Robbie to renew his friendship with Bob Stuart, who had been with him in the cricket team at Highgate School.

There were six matches arranged to be played over eighteen days at clubs within the environs of Buenos Aires. It comes as no surprise that Robbie was one of the party who played in every match. Three of the games were allocated three days and classified as first-class and reported locally as unofficial 'Test' matches. In the first of these the Cahn XI won by ten wickets, thanks to some great bowling from Robbie with match figures of eleven for 85. The next 'Test' was at the Hurlingham Club ground where Robbie outshone everyone with a top score of 71 out of a first-innings total of 189 and ten wickets in the match for 113 runs, but the game was drawn. The final 'Test' followed at the Belgrano Athletic Club where Robbie had match figures of seven for 137 in another draw, giving him a total of 28 wickets out of the 57 taken in the series.

They arrived back at Plymouth on 23 April but the new advertising company was not yet up and running so it was agreed that Robbie should return home and continue to play for Middlesex until he was needed in Nottingham.

* * * * * * *

Only a week after his return from South America, Robbie was in action at Lord's for Middlesex against Leicestershire and for the rest of May he divided his time between cricket and his new employment in Nottingham. He was also able to renew his relationship with Kathleen Knight, despite her disappointment at receiving only one postcard from him during his two-month absence in South America.

Robbie appeared in only three of the next six Middlesex matches. With the bat he scored 140 against Cambridge University at Fenner's, the highest first-class score of his career, but against stronger opposition he did enough to catch the attention of the selectors and was included in the England team for the Test Trial at Lord's. Figures of four for 69 in The Rest's only innings were enough to convince the selectors that he should be included in the England side for the First Test against Australia eight days later. Middlesex were due to play the Australians immediately after the Test Trial but Robbie missed the game as Sir Julien Cahn wanted him in his team to play against the Leicestershire Club and Ground side! The game at West Bridgford was Robbie's first experience of the ground and the lavish way in which Sir Julien entertained his guests.

Robbie returned to Lord's the next day to play for Middlesex against Sussex when his bowling suddenly lost its bite and his match return of one for 119 from 30 overs was disappointing. And it was bowlers at the top of their game that England needed now, facing an Australian batting line-up of Woodfull, Ponsford, Fairfax, Kippax, McCabe and Vic Richardson as well as Don Bradman in outstanding form, having already scored 1,230 runs at an average of 111.82 since arriving in England, including two double centuries and two centuries.

At Trent Bridge Chapman won the toss and Robbie went in to bat at 188 for six, when England were wobbling, and stayed there until close of play with England reaching 241 for eight. There was rain overnight and play could not resume until 2.15 pm when England added another 29 runs for the last two wickets with Robbie scoring 22 of them to reach his unbeaten 50. Australia made a dreadful start to their innings and by the time Chapman brought Robbie into the attack they had already lost Ponsford, Woodfull and Bradman for a mere 16 runs. Fairfax and Kippax were staging a fight-back but Robbie broke the stand by getting Fairfax caught by Hobbs to make it 57 for four, and then had McCabe caught by Hammond bringing the score to 61 for five. Australia ended the day at 140 for eight after Robbie had taken the last two wickets before close of play.

Australia were soon out on Monday morning and after England had rattled up 302 quick runs Australia found themselves batting again before play ended, needing 429 runs to win. Robbie was brought on to bowl with Australia 25 for one and his first three overs went for 17 runs. Chapman didn't call him up again that evening and Australia ended the day at 60 for one. With all day Tuesday available, the pitch looking good, nine wickets in hand and Bradman batting, the target of 369 looked within Australia's reach, particularly when news arrived that Larwood was unable to leave home suffering from acute gastritis. Chapman rotated the bowling between Tate, Tyldesley and Hammond for the first 42 overs of the day, but with only Ponsford gone and Australia 137 for two he reluctantly decided to use Robbie. With the third ball of his third over, Robbie made the breakthrough that England needed when Kippax cut the ball straight to Hammond. When the lunch interval arrived Australia were 198 for three, still needing another 231 to win but with four hours of play left in which to get them and Bradman well set. Soon after Bradman reached his century Tate induced McCabe to pump the ball to mid off and Australia were 229 for four, needing 200 in 195 minutes. Richardson came in to play a supporting role to Bradman who now started to attack Tyldesley and the runs came steadily. In desperation, Chapman turned again to Robbie, who for the past twenty-five overs had been racing around the outfield cutting off boundaries. He immediately forced Bradman on to the defensive and when he delivered the last ball of his third over Bradman read it as a leg-break missing the stumps but, taking no chances, withdrew his bat away from the ball. Instead of spinning harmlessly away, Robbie had sent down his googly which twisted back to strike the off stump. Bradman subsequently claimed that he had picked the delivery as a googly but 'as I moved across to play it my bat got caught in my pad.' Not a very convincing excuse, and if he really believed that he had been beaten by an accident why did he feel the need to threaten Robbie as he passed him on his way back to the pavilion by muttering 'You wait till I get you at Lord's'? The last five wickets fell while adding only 68 runs, Robbie wrapping up Australia's innings and sealing the win by getting Hornibrook caught behind by Duckworth.

Plum Warner was more impressed with Robbie's Ashes debut than some others, saying that he 'bowled finely with seven wickets, including Bradman's, to his credit for 132 runs, had scored a brilliant 50 not out, and, as always, had fielded superbly.' Kathleen Knight certainly was one spectator at Trent Bridge who was impressed by Robbie in his first Ashes Test: 'Walter arranged for me to stay with our mutual friends, Dr and Mrs Cran in Nottingham, and he proposed in their parlour — the fact of taking Don Bradman's wicket having clearly gone to his head — to this day, Don still claims that it was he who was the cause of us getting married!' Their younger son Richard, who lived in Australia in the mid 1960s, recalls that Sir Don was still claiming responsibility 'and always roared with laughter!'

There seemed little doubt that Robbie would retain his place in the England eleven for the Second Test, at Lord's, so he stayed working in Nottingham and declined the opportunity to play in two county matches for Middlesex. But there were changes made by the selectors to the winning team including the replacement of Tyldesley by 39-year-old Jack White, himself one of the selectors and a favourite of Chapman. Larwood and Sutcliffe were both unfit, so at least Robbie was pleased to learn that his Middlesex friend, 'Gubby' Allen had been brought into the side, as well as Duleepsinhji, his former university team-mate. Robbie's accommodation in London was already arranged as his father Vivian had been posted to the Command Pay Office in Malta, so the house in Kingston had been sold and Mabel and Letitia had moved into a flat in St John's Wood with a room for Robbie when he arrived.

Formalities. A.P.F.Chapman introducing K.S.Duleepsinhji to King George V during the Lord's Test of 1930: Robbie is next in line.

As the players gathered at Lord's on the first morning of the Second Test, the England dressing-room became the stage for the 'affair of the caps', a one-act farce starring the chairman of the selectors, 'Shrimp' Leveson Gower, Robbie and Jack Hobbs. Three Middlesex and ex-England players were anxious to replenish their fading England caps and had asked Robbie if he would pick up some new ones for them. He arrived at the ground early and went to the box of new caps in the England dressing-room and slipped three into his bag before going out to have a pre-match net. But his actions had been noticed by another early arrival, Jack Hobbs, who saw an opportunity to play a joke on his younger team-mate. Hobbs emptied the remaining stock into Robbie's bag, then arranged for Leveson Gower to be asked if he could come to the dressing-room and throw any light on the complete disappearance of a boxful of fresh England caps. Robbie was summoned back from the nets and an increasingly irritated Leveson Gower asked all those present if anyone knew what had happened to the thirty caps. As Robbie had taken only three he kept silent, suspecting that someone else must have taken the majority. Then Leveson Gower demanded that the players must open their bags for inspection and, to Robbie's horror, the entire stock of caps fell out of his bag! Leveson Gower was furious that Robbie had not confessed when first asked, but Jack Hobbs quickly calmed the situation by explaining that it was all a practical joke and admitting that he was responsible. Everyone had a good laugh, except perhaps Robbie and Leveson Gower.

England batted first and made a good start, ending the day at 405 for nine, Robbie's contribution a restrained five in thirty minutes while adding 26 with Duleepsinhji who had made a brilliant 173. Within half an hour after play started on Saturday morning England were all out for 425 and by lunch Australia were 96 without loss. Soon after lunch 'Woodfull, with his score at 52 playing forward to Robins, dragged his foot over the crease. Duckworth gathered the ball and swept it back to the stumps, but omitted to remove the bails.' According to *Wisden*, 'that little error cost England dear.' Dear indeed, because Woodfull went on to make 155!

After Ponsford mis-hit White to Hammond at slip, Bradman came in and Chapman persevered with White and Hammond for another eleven overs. He replaced them with six overs from Allen and Tate, and then brought back Hammond. The tea interval arrived; by now twenty-two overs had passed since Bradman had come in but Robbie, who had bamboozled him at Trent Bridge, still had not been used. Warner was not impressed by Chapman's handling of his bowlers and was also surprised that Robbie 'who looked more like getting a wicket than anyone else did not bowl a ball to Bradman until that batsman had made over 50 runs.'

Immediately after tea Chapman at last brought on Robbie but it was too late. In six overs Robbie went for 34 runs, 20 of them to Bradman. Chapman replaced him with White to no avail as he went for 21 runs from four overs, 19 of them to Bradman at a run a ball, and in sheer desperation he turned to the slow left-arm spin of 43-year-old Frank Woolley. His six overs cost 35 runs and 23 of those 36 balls were received by Bradman who scored 22 runs from them. What Chapman had never seemed to realise was that Robbie was the type of bowler who could be expensive at times, but he was always likely to bowl the unplayable ball that would capture a wicket. And so it proved. Yet another 21 overs came and went before he was asked to try again and in his third over, less than ten minutes before close of play, Woodfull went forward misjudging a leg-break and this time Duckworth made no mistake.

Only twelve overs were bowled on Monday morning before Chapman called

*Drinks interval during the Lord's Test of 1930,
with formally dressed waiters and Robbie seated.*

up Robbie. Bradman and Kippax had started defensively and added only
another 19 runs to the overnight score so Robbie fed them a few tempting
deliveries in the hope that they might be lured into making a mistake. It
didn't work although Chapman persevered with him this time for nine
consecutive overs before turning to White, who apart from a couple of
overs from Allen just before lunch, bowled 18 overs before finally getting
Bradman to lift one to Chapman after scoring 254. Australia batted on
and declared at the tea interval leaving England needing 304 to avoid an
innings defeat, and by close of play they were 98 for two.

The following morning England were soon down to 147 for five and it
seemed only a matter of time before Australia would level the series.
Chapman and Allen had other ideas and put on 125 for the sixth wicket
before Allen became Grimmett's fifth victim of the innings. Chapman
batted on to complete his first Test century and added another 57 runs
with Tate. When Robbie came in England had avoided the ignominy of an
innings defeat, so more runs were less important than occupation of the
crease. Chapman's wicket was the key to England's survival and he and
Robbie added another 25 before the captain finally fell. At least they were
now 50 runs in front and Jack White, up next, was no mere tail-ender. They
agreed that White should keep the strike against the seamer Hornibrook
as much as possible, while the quick-footed Robbie would take the spin
of Grimmett. Slowly but surely, he and Robbie added another 18 runs.
Optimistic England supporters believed that if the two batsman had been
able to stay in the middle beyond the tea interval, then Australia might
not have enough time to make the runs they needed to win. Then disaster
struck. Robbie was like a greyhound between wickets but he momentarily
forgot that quick singles were unnecessary at that stage and could leave
his much older partner struggling to reach safety. *Wisden* later reported:
'A foolish call by Robins cost a valuable wicket when White was run out.'

Last man Duckworth was out almost immediately and Australia had more than two hours in which to get the 72 runs needed for victory.

A disconsolate Robbie returned to the pavilion, upset that he may have, unwittingly, made Australia's task easier. Leveson Gower met him on the landing outside the dressing-room and said that he had witnessed some stupid things over fifty years in cricket, but the run-out of White must have been the stupidest. The last thing Robbie expected was an altercation with the chairman of the selectors and his angry response, reminiscent of his father's reply to criticism nearly 30 years before, was to tell Leveson Gower that he resented being criticised by someone obviously 'over-refreshed' straight from the committee-room. Leveson Gower was not noted for his post-lunch temperance and the result, as Ian Peebles later noted, 'had been a heated scene, and in the opinion of those present, the end of Walter's prospects for the current series.'

Seething with anger as he took the field, Robbie must have hoped that Chapman would give him at least a few overs to redeem himself. All credit to his captain, although he really had nothing to lose, because after only seven overs he brought him into the attack and with his fourth ball clean bowled Ponsford. In came Bradman and another four balls later out went Bradman, caught by a delighted Chapman off Tate. According to Warner 'Robins was spinning the ball tremendously' and minutes later he had another wicket when Duckworth caught Kippax. Australia were now 22 for three but, as *Wisden* later reported, 'visions of a remarkable collapse arose but Woodfull, exercising sound generalship by taking most of Robins' bowling himself, tided over an anxious period.' Warner thought that Woodfull had no easy passage: 'Robins got past even Woodfull's cast-iron defence three balls in succession'. McCabe helped his captain weather the storm and despite Robins 'sending down seven almost perfect overs' it was all over by 5 pm.

Despite the final heroics, Robbie suspected that his services would no longer be required by the England selectors. He turned down the opportunity to join Middlesex at Leicester and returned to Nottingham. Probably to counter any suspicions that he was being victimised for the unsavoury events at Lord's, the selectors included Robbie's name among the twelve players invited to Leeds for the Third Test, but in the final selection Dick Tydesley, Lancashire's rotund leggie and nowhere near an allrounder, was preferred. It was a decision that did not find favour with Warner: 'a good many people were reluctant to believe that Tyldesley was a better man in an England team than Robins.' By the first evening of the first day Bradman was 309 not out, having made 100 runs in all three sessions. Robbie was not too disappointed with the twelfth-man role dispensing drinks to perspiring chasers.

Afterwards, Robbie accepted the invitation to go down to Lord's for the traditional Gentlemen versus Players fixture where he was reunited with his old friend Ian Peebles. Captain of the Gentlemen was Percy Chapman, fresh from the Test defeat at Leeds, who continued to prefer other bowlers and Robbie was only used for 18 overs in the match, while Peebles was given 37 and White 28.

Robbie played no first-class cricket in August but he did take time off work to travel south to play a few games for East Molesey. He actually headed both batting and bowling averages for the club that season, closely followed by his father in both categories. MCC were sending a team to tour South Africa that winter and Percy Chapman, who had lost the captaincy of England against Australia for the Fifth Test at The Oval a few weeks earlier, was reinstated as captain for the tour which could explain why the team included White, Tyldesley and Peebles but not Robbie. However, if Robbie had been invited by MCC he might have declined the opportunity, believing that his time would be put to better use if he concentrated on his career in Nottingham and enjoying more football with the Corinthians. It might have been fun to spend a few months in South Africa with his friend Ian Peebles, always assuming that his fiancée Kathleen, who would be studying and revising for her LRAM examinations, had given her approval!

The football season would begin in less than a month and Robbie would be able to spend Saturdays at Crystal Palace and other football grounds, as part of well-earned weekend breaks from his total five days a week commitment to the marketing and advertising of the products and services of the Nottingham Furnishing Company. And after celebrating Kathleen's examination success, there was the wedding of his elder sister to 'Pip' Piper, his old University football team-mate, to look forward to.

Robbie and Kathleen in London at the time of their engagement.

Chapter Five

Part-Time Cricket

The 1930/31 football season was soon under way and between 11 October and 13 December, Robbie played in every Corinthian first-eleven match, as well as making another appearance for Nottingham Forest in a friendly at Oxford University. On Christmas Day he played again for the professionals at home in a Second Division match against Reading. On New Year's Day he was in Scotland for the traditional game with Queen's Park at Hampden Park, which the Corinthians won 2-0. Robbie played in nine of the next ten games and then it was time for the Easter tour, this year to Switzerland with a game in Berne and another in Zurich.

Returning to England there was just enough time for Robbie to play one more game, his twenty-fifth before he began to make preparations for the 'Big Day' in less than a fortnight — his marriage to Kathleen Knight at All Souls, Langham Place, just off Oxford Street in central London, on 23 April. There was a huge crowd present and after the service the happy couple drove to Highgate to see Robbie's old headmaster and mentor Dr Johnston, who had been unable to attend the wedding due to illness. Returning from their honeymoon at Babbacombe in Devon, they moved into a small detached house in the Nottingham suburb of Edwalton.

Kathleen and Robbie outside All Souls, Langham Place in central London after their wedding on St George's Day 1931.

Two weeks later Robbie was at Lord's playing for MCC in the opening game against Surrey. (He had been elected to MCC membership during the close season.) This would be one of only seven first-class matches he would play in the summer of 1931. It seems that Sir Julien Cahn was once again happy to encourage Robbie to play in all of the Middlesex early matches to see if he could earn his place in the England line-up for the Test at Lord's at the end of June. But when July and August arrived Robbie was expected to give priority as usual to the fixtures at West Bridgford and elsewhere for the Cahn XI. That didn't stop him dashing down to East Molesey whenever he could and in 1931 he was able to make ten appearances for the club.

Plum Warner had taken over from Leveson Gower as chairman of the Test selectors and his faith in Robbie's allround ability never wavered. New Zealand were the visitors to England but were allocated only one Test, their first in England, starting on 27 June at Lord's, and Robbie was selected. England were 188 for six at 6.20 pm on the first day in reply to New Zealand's 224 when Ian Peebles was surprisingly sent in as nightwatchman. Two runs later he was stumped for nought and stumps were drawn with England 190 for seven. Peebles' nought stayed up on the pre-electronic scoreboard all Sunday and most of the second day as Gubby Allen and Les Ames both made hundreds in a stand of 246 and he ruefully remembered how his embarrassment had been intensified:

> This afforded the two Walters, Hammond and Robins, the most exquisite boyish pleasure. All through Monday they kept enquiring of each other what the last chap had made — who was he? — Hobbs, Sutcliffe, Tyldesley? No, Peebles.

Jardine had been unimpressed by the jesting and Peebles recalled that on arriving on Tuesday Douglas drew me aside and said it might all be very funny but it was what one would describe as rather 'fourth form'. When Walter Robins arrived, Douglas spoke to him on the matter but unfortunately did so with his back to the glass door leading to the balcony. The effect of his rebuke was rather lessened by an admiring group standing behind him waving encouragement to the accused interspersed with some less courteous gestures!

However, Jardine had need of his two bowlers to take matters more seriously when New Zealand made a fighting comeback in their second innings and the England captain asked Robbie to bowl 37 overs in a spin partnership with Peebles who bowled 43 overs before the match ended in a draw.

It was obvious that New Zealand were a better side than had been expected and two more Tests were quickly arranged, although the selectors could no longer call upon Robbie to take his place in the England eleven. Apart from the Gentlemen and Players match at Lord's in the middle of July, the rest of the summer it was mainly one-day cricket for the Cahn XI for which he scored 1,256 runs, including four centuries, and took 125 wickets. Robbie and Kathleen had, as we have seen, now moved to Nottingham and she recorded her impressions:

> This, of course, was our first year at Nottingham and Sir Julien, Lady

Cahn and the side were delightful to us. Cricket at Loughboro' Road was good fun and the wives sat in old-fashioned chairs with tops like a sentry box, very warm and draught free. Better even was cricket at Stanford Hall, where the hospitality was unlimited and the weather always seemed to be fine. Lunch and tea were served in a large marquee with wonderful food and all manner of drinks, also one could swim or play a few holes of golf if the cricket was dull, which it rarely was.

There was only a two-week break before the start of the football season. Robbie was a regular in the Corinthians' team for the first thirteen matches. In their first year as a married couple, Robbie and Kathleen were determined to be at both the Knight and Robins Christmas festivities. This meant no football for Robbie for 14 days but he did manage to get down to the South Coast on 28 December to play against Brighton and Hove Albion and on New Year's Eve played a part in the 2-1 defeat of Clapton Orient. He played in another eight games and then went on the Corinthians' Easter tour to Ireland. He was back in England by the beginning of April but for him the season was over as he concentrated on office work until the start of the 1932 cricket season.

His usual agreement with Sir Julien Cahn continued and he was free to take leave of absence from office duties and play first-class cricket throughout May and June. This suited Warner and the England selectors very well, as it meant that Robbie would be prepared for the only Test of the season, against 'All-India'. After the opening game for MCC against Yorkshire, the previous season's champions, in which he took five for 61 in their only innings, he played four more games for Middlesex before Jardine was pleased to welcome him back into his bowling line-up against the Indians at Lord's. But in this Test it was Robbie's batting that impressed, not because of the number of runs he scored, 21 and 30, but because of the support he gave to Ames in a 63-run seventh-wicket stand in the first innings and in the second, a 53-run stand, also for the seventh wicket, this time with Paynter. There was still time for one more game in the south, at Tunbridge Wells where he took six for 45 in Kent's first innings and gave every indication that, if he had been free to carry on playing for Middlesex, he would have been certain to have taken 100 first-class wickets in a season for the second time.

But Robbie was not back in Nottingham for long before he and Kathleen were off with Sir Julien once again on a five-day tour of Denmark. Meanwhile, Warner and the selectors were busy trying to put a balanced team together for Jardine to take to Australia and New Zealand for the MCC winter tour and the Ashes series. At the beginning of August, Robbie received his invitation but the selection could not have come at a more inconvenient time. Kathleen had just announced that they were expecting their first child which was due to arrive early in March 1933, several weeks before the MCC tourists would arrive back in England. Obviously, the invitation had to be turned down, although Sir Julien Cahn had come forward with the suggestion that Robbie could go for part of the tour and return early at Sir Julien's expense. MCC did not give Robbie that option and told him that 'we have written to Sir Julien in response to his generous offer'.

The Robins family were delighted at the news of the expected arrival of a new member and cricket at East Molesey in the summer of 1932 was 'very much of a family affair these days' as described in the Winter Annual of *The Cricketer* when it published the club's season averages for 1932 which included Robbie, his father, his uncle, his brother and his brother-in-law:

Batting	I	N.O	Runs	H.S.	Ave
R.W.V.Robins	11	0	489	92	44.45
W.V.H.Robins	8	0	173	34	21.62
V.H.Robins	19	1	284	62	15.77
H.F.Piper	20	0	256	100	12.80
Lt Col V.I.Robins	35	10	156	22	6.24

Bowling	O	M	Runs	Wkt	Ave
R.W.V.Robins	137	22	366	53	6.90
V.H.Robins	225	45	556	65	8.55
H.F.Piper	239	76	550	58	9.48

With the summer now over, Robbie looked forward to playing football in the fiftieth-anniversary season of the Corinthians. He was asked to play on either the right or left wing and sometimes even moved to inside-right as the club tried to find a winning combination in time for the FA Cup tie against West Ham United on 14 January. But he had to rule himself out of contention for a place in the fixture when the Corinthians decided, for the first time in their history, that they wanted the team to train together at Crystal Palace every evening from Monday 9 January to Friday 13 January when Robbie would be working in Nottingham.

* * * * * * *

Robbie and Kathleen had moved from Nottingham to a small house at Burnham in Buckinghamshire in time for the birth of their daughter in March 1933. As Kathleen explains in her memoir: 'Walter was beginning to miss his Middlesex cricket. The country-house flavour of Julien Cahn's cricket was not enough.' There was very little competition and in the three seasons since Robbie had accepted Sir Julien's offer of employment, the cricket team had played 115 matches, winning 62 and losing only four. Understanding her husband better than anyone and his motto — 'Make a good game of it' — Kathleen sympathised with Robbie's dilemma: 'I can understand his irritation conflicting with his feelings of gratitude for Sir Julien's hospitality and generosity.'

Robbie's dissatisfaction with the quality of cricket was increased by his frustration at being unable to test his skills to the full by taking part in a whole Test series or another complete championship season. Just when Robbie's thought may have been turning to seriously seeking alternative employment in London, which would give him freedom to play more first-class cricket, once again Sir Julien had an ace up his sleeve — another all-expenses-paid tour abroad, this time to North America in August and September. That meant that all the Cahn players would have to cut short their season in England after July, but as far as Sir Julien was concerned, there was no difference between his employees being released for a series of matches overseas or playing two or three times a week for him in England. But for Robbie it would do nothing to further his Test and county cricket ambitions. However, his employment had always been subject to his being able to take extended leave during May, June and the first few days of July, to play for Middlesex, MCC and, perhaps, England, returning occasionally for games in Nottingham when required. Sir Julien realised that he would need to make concessions if he was going to keep his star player, and so that period of release was extended to include the whole month of July. This meant that not only could Robbie hope to play in two Test matches, but also much more county cricket for Middlesex. For the time being, at least, this pushed those doubts identified by Kathleen, to one side.

But, in practice, the arrangement did not provide quite as many opportunities to play first-class cricket as Robbie had expected. From the start of their 1933 season in April until they sailed for Canada on 12 August, the Cahn XI played two or three times a week for a total of 35 matches, with Robbie playing in many of them. During the same period Middlesex played 19 matches, in which Robbie appeared only eight times. He also played in the first two Test matches against the West Indies and once for MCC against Kent, but these matches did not clash with Middlesex fixtures, so in effect, he played in less than half of the Middlesex matches for which he presumed he would be available. And this was because he had been called back to Nottingham to play country-house cricket far more frequently than he had anticipated. Sir Julien presumably believed that he had honoured his side of the bargain as Robbie appeared for Middlesex more often than in 1931 and 1932, and had been available for the first two Tests. On the other hand, it seems unlikely that Robbie would have been satisfied with the way the season had gone, and thoughts of seeking new employment may have resurfaced.

In his eight appearances for Middlesex, Robbie's best bowling figures were seven for 36 in Hampshire's second innings in the opening match at Lord's, and five for 102 in Somerset's first innings in his last county match before the First Test. His batting once again was more impressive, including his only first-class century of the summer, 106 against Kent. The new chairman of England's selection committee was Lord Hawke. He had stepped in to replace Plum Warner who had declined the MCC invitation to continue, saying he was 'in need of a rest from any sort of cricket responsibility'. The real reason, of course, was that Warner believed he had a far greater responsibility — the future of cricket itself. Throughout 1933 he worked behind the scenes to outlaw Bodyline from English cricket before the Australians arrived in 1934, and conspired to take the captaincy of England away from Jardine. Hawke, like many others in the corridors of power at Lord's, saw no reason why Jardine, the hero of the hour who had

Sir Julien Cahn's XI in 1933. Standing (l to r): –, C.R.N.Maxwell, G.F.Summers, H.R.Munt, S.D.Rhodes, E.P.Solbé, T.B.Reddick, J.R.Gunn (umpire). Seated: D.P.B.Morkel, R.W.V.Robins, F.C.W.Newman, Sir J.Cahn, –, F.J.Seabrook, G.F.H.Heane.

returned from Australia with the Ashes, should not continue as England's captain in the series against the West Indies. It was, indeed, a popular choice and Jardine received a standing ovation from the public, and most MCC members in the pavilion, when he went out to bat at Lord's in the First Test of the 1933 season.

Even without the benefits of Warner's patronage, Robbie was sure of a place in the England line-up at Lord's and he repaid the trust of Hawke and Jardine with a fine spell of bowling. Play on the first day was seriously reduced by rain and when the West Indies finally started their reply to England's 296 all out, they quickly collapsed to 55 for six before the close of play on Monday evening with Robbie having taken two of their wickets. When play resumed on the third and final day Jardine soon brought Robbie into the attack and he took all of the remaining wickets while West Indies could only add another 42 runs. His final figures were six for 32, his best Test return. Following on, the West Indies improved until Robbie had Barrow lbw at 56 for two, and with Headley falling to Gubby Allen after reaching his half-century, the rest of the wickets fell to Macaulay and Verity to give England an innings victory.

Immediately the Lord's Test was over on the Tuesday evening, Robbie and the West Indian tourists travelled up to Nottingham where he would face them again in a two-day match for Sir Julien Cahn's XI that began the next day. It would be two weeks before he was back playing first-class cricket and he managed to fit in only two county matches before the start of the Second Test, at Old Trafford.

Robbie's performance in the First Test had guaranteed his place in the England team for the Second Test but he might have wished afterwards that he had been left out. He conceded more than four runs an over in the West Indies' first innings during which Barrow and Headley added 200 for the second wicket and he suffered from a strained stomach muscle in the last two hours of play on the first day. It was in England's only innings that Robbie may also have preferred to have been somewhere else. The West Indian all-rounder, Learie Constantine, had not been released for the First Test by Nelson, the Lancashire League club where he was employed as the resident professional. But after further negotiations, agreement had been reached for his appearance at Old Trafford and it was an opportunity for him to join Martindale, the other fast bowler, and for them to give England a taste of Bodyline. The *Wisden* report tells part of the story:

> No account of this Test match would be complete without reference to the method of attack adopted by Martindale and Constantine for the West Indies and Clark for England [in the West Indies second innings]. The game at Lord's had passed by without any of the fast leg-theory bowling with a packed leg field which had caused such trouble in Australia the previous winter. At Manchester, however, we saw a lot of it and, judging by the opinions afterwards expressed, it met with little commendation.

Martindale and Constantine directed much of their version of Bodyline at Douglas Jardine 'with unflagging zeal' and *Wisden* thought it to his great credit 'that he played it probably better than any other man in the world was capable of doing, while putting together' his first-ever Test century. The almanack added that although Jardine showed that 'it was possible to meet it without suffering physical injury or losing his wicket through any impatient or wild strike,' it did not, however, 'make the sight of it any more welcome, and many of those who were watching it for the first time must have come to the conclusion that, while strictly within the law, it was not nice.'

It certainly was not 'nice' to be on the receiving end of the Bodyline bowling from Martindale and Constantine, but *Wisden* makes no mention of the part Robbie played while in the firing line when he joined Jardine at 234 for six near the end of the second day, with England still 141 runs behind. Jardine attempted to re-assure his new partner with the statement: 'This is absolutely no problem, Robins.' After ducking and dodging for an over or two, Robbie told his captain: 'It may be no problem for you up there at 6 foot 3 inches, but you want to come down to 5 foot 7 inches!' The pair survived until stumps with Jardine on 68 and Robins on six.

The next morning the onslaught continued but both batsmen refused to be intimidated and took England past the West Indies total while adding 140 runs for the seventh wicket with Jardine reaching three figures and Robbie his half-century, England's next top scorer with 55, but without a single boundary. Ironically, it wasn't a bouncer that finally ended Robbie's innings but an attempt on his part to take advantage of a brief respite while Martindale and Constantine were rested, and go down the wicket to attack the spin bowling of 'Puss' Achong and being stumped by Barrow. An event celebrated by a disappointed Robbie on his return to the pavilion with the statement: 'Fancy being stumped off a bloody chinaman!' which was later said to have given life to that term for a left-armer's googly. However, Robbie always denied being the originator and said he had only repeated a similar cry of frustration made by his friend 'Patsy' Hendren two years earlier in Trinidad: 'Fancy being bowled by a bloody chinaman!' after Achong, making his Test debut, had bowled him when Hendren was well on his way to another century.

There were still four more Middlesex matches before the ship sailed for Canada but Robbie featured in none of them. Instead, he was kept busy back in Nottingham seeing that the team was fully prepared for the tour ahead of them. But he would have particularly enjoyed the last of the matches for Sir Julien. It was at Wolstanton against Staffordshire, the county of his birth, and he took the opportunity to confirm that the quality of Staffordshire cricket had been passed on to him by his father and cracked a brilliant 148. Three days later, all the players selected for the tour were gathered together at Claridge's Hotel in London for a farewell lunch.

The squad was another collection of varied talents, experience and inexperience, similar to that taken to Argentina. In addition to Robbie, four members had toured two years before: George Heane, Harold Munt, 'Lofty' Newman and Stuart Rhodes. This time there were three other players younger than Robbie as well as Stuart Rhodes: these were Cecil Maxwell, 20, who had joined the Cahn empire straight from Brighton College the year before; Paul Gibb, 20, who had started playing for Cahn earlier that year; and Tommy Reddick, 21, who had moved to Nottingham in 1932 to study the methods of furniture manufacture at one of Cahn's upholstery factories before taking up a position at a large Jay's store in Manchester.

There were three other Test cricketers in the party, in addition to Robbie. From the Dominions there was Roger Blunt, the New Zealander who also worked in the advertising department, and Denys Morkel from South Africa who Sir Julien was helping to establish a motor business in Nottingham. From England, via Scotland, there was Robbie's old and trusted friend Ian Peebles, although for this trip it was Kathleen who was trusting him to bring her husband back safe and sound. Making up the final number of fourteen players were Edward Solbé, 30, a county player for Kent back in 1924, and Gerald Summers who had moved up to Nottingham a year earlier after several seasons as a regular with Surrey seconds. Last, but by no means least, was a journalist from the London *Evening Standard* who was also a talented amateur cricketer, the 26-year-old Jim Swanton, who explained his presence on the tour: 'Through a chance remark when playing cricket at Sir Julien Cahn's house, I found myself invited by that gregarious sporting millionaire.'

During the farewell lunch at Claridge's on 11 August, J.H.Thomas, Secretary of State for Dominion Affairs, proposed the toast to 'Cricket, Canada and the Team' and the Lord Mayor of Nottingham spoke of Sir Julien's service to the game of cricket, so the tour was no lightweight matter. After a night at the hotel, the team, together with Lady Cahn, her father and mother and her aunt, sailed from Southampton. They landed at Quebec on 18 August and the nine games in Canada provided easy wins for the visitors and it was expected that the opposition in the United States would offer even less of a challenge.

In Chicago the first match against a Chicago XV was in a public park with baseball games going on all around. According to Ian Peebles: 'Characteristically Walter Robins was soon in the midst of one of these where he was made very welcome, and astonished the players with his bare-handed fielding.' John Warr rather later commented: 'It is probably as one of the greatest fielders in the history of the game that he would choose to be remembered. As a naturally good runner and mover, his bow legs seemed to give him a low centre of gravity. He could swoop and pick up the ball in one breathtaking movement.' This game was repeated the next day and then the tourists spent a day at the World's Fair after which they accepted an invitation from 'associates' of Al Capone, overlord of a bootlegging cartel from Canada to Florida, to spend an evening seeing something of the city's underworld nightlife, including visiting various 'speakeasies'. They left the next day for New York on the famous train, *The Twentieth Century Limited*, and arrived in the 'Big Apple' twenty hours later. There were three matches to play, then the party sailed from New York to Bermuda where they were due to play five matches in five days, all of them at the Police Recreation Club ground at Prospect. There the opposition was expected to be much stronger with all the opposition teams restricted to only eleven players.

The first match was drawn but next day there was a confrontation that must have hardened Robbie's resolve to look for a new job when he returned to Britain. The ground was full at the time scheduled for the match to begin against the St George's Cricket Club, but there was no sign of Sir Julien. The crowd began to get restless and Robbie decided to take over and toss-up with the other skipper to get the game started. By the time Sir Julien arrived the game was in progress and his side were not doing very well, having lost their first three wickets for only 44 runs. Sir Julien was fuming at the prospect of defeat and refused to be placated by Robbie, even after a stand of 97 for the fourth wicket which restored some pride, only to see the next six wickets fall for 68 runs, including Sir Julien bowled first ball. Despite no opposing team reaching 150 in any innings in any match on the tour to date, a target of 210 looked within the reach of the Bermudians and it took all the skill and cunning of Robbie's five for 32 and Peebles' four for 21 to ensure that they got nowhere near the winning total.

Sir Julien was on time for the next match, which was another victory for the tourists, and then, being advised that the opposition would be stronger than any of the teams they had faced so far, he decided to sit out and socialise for the last two games against Somerset, the best club on the island and then a representative team, an 'All-Bermuda XI', leaving Robbie to captain the side — and take responsibility for any defeat, no doubt! Cricket history was made in game against Somerset when Cahn's XI became 'the first white side to play a club of black men, and to mark the occasion a public holiday was declared.' The game was played in front of a massive crowd, some perched in the branches of trees, and included troops from the British Army garrison. Gambling was rife. Robbie won the toss and elected to bat, seemingly a good choice with the team 66 for two at lunch. Then Somerset brought Arthur Simons on to bowl and at fast-medium pace, pitching on the leg-stump and hitting the off, he took seven for 19 reducing the visitors to 85 all out. Robbie decided to open the bowling himself with Peebles at the other end and soon nine wickets were down for 70. The game was unexpectedly held up while drinks were brought on to the field by a sergeant of the Northumberland Fusiliers who said to Peebles, 'For gawd's sake get this over, sir, the troops have got every button they could raise on you.' But twelve more runs were quickly added and with only four runs needed to win Robbie was hit high over mid off. George Heane started to run from deep extra cover and measured the flight of the ball perfectly, which he caught a foot over his head. The joyful soldiers poured onto the field and carried Heane shoulder high to the pavilion, where Sir Julien was also seized, 'somewhat to his alarm, and borne aloft likewise'. With all this excitement, it is perhaps not surprising Swanton commented that 'Walter Robins always said this was the most thrilling game he ever saw or played in.'

Defeat was also only narrowly avoided in the final game of the tour and, as Sir Julien had hoped, he and his players could sail home undefeated.

There was time for a few days in New York before leaving on the *R.M.S.Aquitania.* As Peebles was fully occupied with an American actress on the voyage — the fair sex were a hazard for international sportsmen, Robbie included, long before the twenty-first century — Robbie perhaps had more time alone to ponder on his future. He concluded that this must be outside the Nottingham Furnishing Company and away from the generosity of Sir Julien Cahn which came at a price he now felt unable to pay.

Inevitably, not all the scores of the Cahn matches have survived, so it is difficult to summarise his cricket with the eleven. Robbie is known, however, to have scored 4,614 runs at 30, and taken 720 wickets at close to 11 for the side. His highest score was 148 against Staffordshire at Porthill in 1933 and his best bowling return eight for 22 against Hampstead C.C. at Hampstead in 1932.

Chapter Six

Captain of Middlesex

When Robbie arrived home from America he discovered that Kathleen had already been taking positive steps to help resolve his employment/ cricket dilemma. An offer awaited him: 'an interest in the family firm of insurance brokers that had been started by my father, Stafford Knight and Co, connected with Lloyds, with whom my father and two of my brothers were underwriters.' Having already proved himself a successful salesman working in the advertising department of the Nottingham Furniture Company, Robbie was now going to sell general insurance on half commission with a minimum guarantee of £400 p.a.: his commitment was to be flexible enough to ensure that he would be able to play full-time first-class cricket during the summer months.

Advising Sir Julien Cahn of his intention to sever his connection with the Nottingham Furniture Company, Robbie was summoned to his employer's office. After thanking Robbie for all his help and support over the past three years, Sir Julien had a more practical way of expressing his gratitude. On his desk in front of him was a pile of correspondence which he picked up and passed across to Robbie. They were copies of letters that had been sent by Sir Julien to the many furniture manufacturers around London, introducing Robbie and saying that unless they placed their insurances through him, their relationship with the purchasing department of Nottingham Furnishing Company 'could be reviewed'. Insurances on highly combustible products is expensive and Robbie never forgot this exceptional act of kindness that set up his insurance career and in his first year alone saw him earn £2,700 in commission. It seems that he took to the arcane world of insurance as to the manor born.

But first of all he had to establish himself in business and this left little time to train and play for the Corinthians whose new football season was well underway. That winter he played only five games for the first eleven, sometimes as inside forward, other times on the wing, and turned down the invitation to go on the club's Easter tour of Germany, Holland and Denmark.

Robbie's priority was following up and converting all the leads supplied by Sir Julien into contracts so that his office desk was clear before the start of the 1934 cricket season. With that achieved by the end of April he was delighted to accept Sir Julien's invitation to play at West Bridgford in a pair of back-to-back two-day matches against Derbyshire and Leicestershire. And this time it did not mean sacrificing a first-class county match, as he could go straight from Nottingham to Northampton where Middlesex began their season the next day. Ian Peebles joined Robbie at West

Bridgford where they launched another fruitful partnership, and in the first four Middlesex matches shared all ten wickets of Northamptonshire's second innings and all ten wickets of Sussex's first innings at Lord's. In all four matches they had captured 47 wickets between them but when the Australians came to Lord's their magic failed. The tourists hit 345 with Bradman making 160 of them, although it was Peebles who finally had him caught before they went on to beat Middlesex by ten wickets in two days. Robbie's contribution was with the bat, scoring 65 and adding 142 with Hendren for the fourth wicket in the Middlesex first innings.

Robbie had already hit three half-centuries as well as taking 24 wickets so it came as no surprise that he was included in the Test Trial six days later. His disappointing performance, no wickets and 90 runs from 25 overs and a total of 24 runs from his two innings meant that he was not asked to join the England team for the First Test at Nottingham where the allrounder role went to 40-year-old George Geary.

Middlesex were without Peebles for the next three games and Robbie struggled to recover any of his earlier form, taking only eleven wickets and averaging 15 with the bat. He did score an impressive 64 for the Gentlemen of England against the Australians at Lord's but again his bowling failed to impress and he was not called for the Second Test at Lord's. At the end of June, business commitments brought the withdrawal of the Middlesex captain, Tom Enthoven, for the rest of the season and, with Nigel Haig still unavailable, the Middlesex committee asked Robbie to step in for the next match at Trent Bridge. As luck would have it, Peebles could return to the side and this seemed a perfect opportunity for Robbie to demonstrate his suitability to fill the role as the next Middlesex captain. Sharing eight wickets Larwood and Voce went quickly through the Middlesex first innings of 218, but when Nottinghamshire batted Robbie soon dispensed with his own opening quick bowlers and called up Peebles to bowl from one end while he bowled from the other. The strategy worked and by close of play on the first day Nottinghamshire were 105 for six. The next morning Robbie continued with this attack and Nottinghamshire were soon all out for 158. Out of the 60 overs bowled in that innings, Robbie and Peebles had bowled 53 and taken four wickets each with the other two being run-outs. Batting again, Middlesex were soon skittled out for 113 with Voce taking seven for 62, suggesting that the wicket had now swung back to favouring pace rather than spin. But Nottinghamshire now needed 173 to win and Robbie scented victory. He gave Gray and Hulme one over each and then returned to the same combination of Peebles and himself which he thought would soon win the match. But it all went wrong and as Robbie persevered with his leg-spin attack for 39 overs out of 61, Harris and Hardstaff added 74 for the second wicket and then Carr joined Hardstaff for a partnership of 86 to win the match by eight wickets.

Details of the defeat soon reached Lord's and Nigel Haig was persuaded to return as captain immediately while Robbie took the opportunity to have a break for the rest of July to concentrate on business matters that needed attention while enjoying a few games at East Molesey. He was back in the Middlesex side at the beginning of August for a couple of games but without much success and his record for the season, 685 runs at an average of 31.00 and 42 wickets for 29.61 each, with no Test appearances, was not the result he had been expecting.

Work now occupied him full-time until the start of the new football season but his first run-out was not until 6 October when he made an emotional return to Highgate School with the Corinthians 'A' eleven, helping them beat the school 5-0. He played only four games for the first eleven, not wishing to travel to away matches until his last game of the season on 9 February and a month later celebrated the birth of his first son, Robert Victor Charles, on 13 March at their recently built new home at Burnham Beeches. Robbie had bought a piece of land in Green Lane, about half-a-mile from their first house in Burnham village. Its plot occupied about three-quarters of an acre with farmland at the back and views over the golf course. The house was built to Kathleen's design with five bedrooms, three reception rooms and two bathrooms. There was a big lawn at the front with room for a cricket net, and another at the back, later converted into a tennis court.

Prosperous times. The Robins family's new house under construction in Green Lane, Burnham, in 1934. At one time it had two cricket nets.

Then Robbie was clearing the decks for what appeared to be a make-or-break cricket season. What he did not know was that, behind the scenes, the Middlesex committee were seeking a new captain now that Nigel Haig had finally retired and Tom Enthoven was unable to commit to more than an occasional appearance. Enthoven had been inclined to be somewhat lackadaisical as a captain and on more than one occasion had accidentally shown Robbie how not to look after his team. During an early game of the 1933 season against Gloucestershire Wally Hammond had been thrashing the ball all over Lord's when the tea interval arrived with the new ball long overdue. According to Ian Peebles, as the Middlesex players trudged off the field Robbie said to Enthoven: 'I suppose you're keeping the new ball till after tea?' His harassed captain halted in his tracks: 'Oh, dammit,' he sighed, 'I'd forgotten all about it.'

That was just the style of captaincy that the Middlesex committee was determined to change. Robbie was an obvious choice, but there were concerns about placing the fortunes of the team in the hands of a player whose experience of captaincy was as a brilliant schoolboy cricketer leading by example, and as right-hand man to Sir Julien Cahn helping him steer his band of mercenaries to a series of victories against weaker opponents in the world of country-house cricket in England and club cricket overseas. And of course the defeat at Nottingham the summer before when, trusted to lead the team for the first time, some thought he threw the game away by stubbornly keeping the bowling in his own and Peebles' hands when he should have considered the alternatives much sooner, had not helped his case.

In Robbie's favour was the growing sense within the committee of the need for a new direction in the selection of players, away from reliance on talented amateurs. The committee had taken a revolutionary decision and agreed to pay for winter coaching for seven young professionals at the indoor school run by ex-Middlesex player Jack Durston, and were also paying the living costs in London for the young Norfolk allrounder Bill Edrich while he completed his qualification for Middlesex. Looking to the future, the committee took a deep breath and chose Robins, now 28, as their new captain and it would prove to be the best decision they could have made. David Lemmon later commented: 'His athletic example and his positive and immediate decisions transformed the Middlesex side, roused it from its sense of gloomy despondency and made it play with the dynamism that its captain imposed on it, for, in truth, he left his imprint upon a generation of cricketers.'

The group of players that he inherited was filled with professionals, including the veterans Jack Hearne, aged 44, and Patsy Hendren, aged 46, supported by the experienced wicketkeeper Fred Price, brilliant fielder and reliable batsman George Hart, the leg-spinner Jim Sims, Arsenal footballer and fast bowler Joe Hulme, and big-hitter and fast bowler 'Big Jim' Smith. Younger players seeking regular places included Laurie Gray, Len Muncer and Jack Young. Of the amateurs that might be available Robbie would later recall that, as soon as his appointment was announced, his telephone suddenly started ringing with offers from amateurs who fancied playing an occasional first-class match from time to time, but only John Human, a tall, attacking batsman could play the whole season. He could expect occasional appearances from experienced amateurs like George Newman, Gubby Allen, Ian Peebles and 'Tuppy' Owen-Smith, and Tom Enthoven would fill in as captain if and when Robbie was on duty for the England Test team.

The 1935 season was the summer of the 'leather jackets' at Lord's when crane-fly larvae ravaged the playing surface and in the process of destroying them, the chemicals used also removed much of the grass so that batting became a hazardous business. Low scores meant that many matches were finished in two days and no side succeeded in scoring over 200 runs in the fourth innings. Middlesex started their season by winning the first two matches, thanks to some inspired bowling at times from Robbie himself and a couple of captain's innings that turned potential defeat into victory. Needing 57 runs to beat Lancashire, the first five wickets went down for only 30 when Robbie came in to take control and with an unbeaten 19 see them through to win without further loss. He faced the same situation four days later against Worcestershire when, needing 100 runs to win, Middlesex had reached only 70 with the loss of six wickets before Robbie entered and steered them through to their target with an unbeaten 16. Inspired by their captain's fighting spirit — Pelham Warner thought his 'activity and evident enjoyment of every moment of a cricket match had a stimulating effect on his comrades, and on the spectators' — Middlesex players now began to believe that they could maintain a genuine challenge for the Championship and they went on to win eleven of their 24 matches.

International duties had meant that Robbie had to miss five county matches. Warner had returned to the England selection committee with Perrin and Higson to act for the next two years to allow continuity of ideas and establish the body of the team which was to visit Australia in 1936/37. This meant that Robbie, who had been ignored during the Ashes series the summer before, was back in the frame, and his county form in the run-up to the First Test against South Africa at Trent Bridge ensured that he was once more in England colours. His batting wasn't required before England declared at 384 for seven with Wyatt, the England captain, scoring 149. There was rain at the weekend and the pace of Nichols saw the visitors having to follow-on 164 behind and end the day at 17 for one. On the final day rain prevented a ball being bowled and Robbie could only look forward to making a bigger contribution at Lord's, four weeks later.

No doubt Warner and the other selectors were expecting the same when they sat down with Wyatt to discuss their options but it was not so straightforward. Warner later wrote:

> The choice of this team involved the longest [selectors'] meeting of my experience. It began at 11 o'clock in the morning and did not end until nearly seven. The point at issue was whether Robins or Mitchell should play. The selectors were unanimous in urging the claims of Robins, and Wyatt, for his part, was emphatic in urging Mitchell. Following Lord Harris's method we adjourned for luncheon, but after luncheon Wyatt was as insistent as ever. Then came tea, but Wyatt still favoured Mitchell. We pointed out that Mitchell, good bowler as he was, had been a complete failure against the Australians in the previous summer, and that in no sense could he be compared with Robins either as batsman or fieldsman; and that Robins, indeed, was one of the best all-round cricketers in England.

The argument continued but Wyatt remained obstinate and 'no comparison of previous performances, however, could convince him, and in the end we gave way.' England went on to lose the match by 157 runs and Mitchell was a disappointment with only three wickets for 54 runs apiece.

The selectors replaced Mitchell with Sims at Leeds but he fared no better and Robbie was brought back for the Fourth Test at Old Trafford. England batted first and were soon down to 141 for five when Robbie joined Leyland. As he usually did in such situations, Robbie responded by attacking the bowlers and the pair hit 105 runs in 75 minutes: Warner said 'Robins was very quick on his feet and made some beautiful off-drives.' After the dismissal of Leyland he went on to add another 58 with Verity and complete his first Test century, reaching 108 before being bowled by Bell at 338 for eight. South Africa were set a target of 271 runs to win on the last day at 72 an hour, but made no effort to reach the target after losing their first two wickets to Robbie for 103. England needed a win at The Oval to square the series and Wyatt put South Africa in to bat on a perfect pitch. Mitchell and Siedle reached 116 without loss but immediately after lunch Robbie struck with two quick wickets. Wyatt soon returned to his pace bowlers and Robbie was not called upon again while the total rose from 139 to 261. After the combined total for the first two innings exceeded a thousand runs the game inevitably rolled to a third consecutive draw, although Robbie had the last laugh by taking the final two wickets to fall in the match.

That autumn MCC decided to send a side of up-and-coming young players on a full tour of New Zealand, preceded by a series of six matches in Australia against each State and an Australian XI. Ten of the 14 players were under 30, and it was hoped that the experience would indicate to the selectors if any of them would be suitable prospects for the Ashes tour twelve months later. Wyatt was asked to captain the side but he declined. It would have been an ideal opportunity for Robbie but he could not afford six months away from business at that time and the position was filled by Errol Holmes of Surrey. Holmes carried out his responsibilities as captain exactly as MCC had hoped, both on and off the field in Australia, going a long way to help heal the wounds inflicted by Bodyline. Many people saw him as an ideal candidate for the position as the next captain of the full England team.

Back in England that winter, Robbie went with the Corinthians 'A' side which beat Highgate School 7-0 on 16 November, but played only one first-team match. This game, against Cardiff City, was his one-hundredth such appearance for the Corinthians. He was one of only 18 players who had made 100 or more appearances for the First XI between the club's formation in 1882 and its disappearance as a separate entity in 1939.

Having lost three Test series in a row, the England selectors decided to replace Wyatt with a new captain in 1936: there were a number of county captains from which they could choose. Whoever was picked, his performance in the three Test series against India would be closely monitored with a view to selection as captain for the next tour of Australia and New Zealand. But there was a surprise wild card. Gubby Allen announced that he had made arrangements to play more often that summer, although he would serve under Robbie's captaincy for Middlesex. A trial match was arranged at Lord's before the First Test and, not wishing to indicate that a decision had been made, the selectors changed the nomenclature from 'England v The Rest' to 'North v South'.

In the weeks before the trial, Middlesex played eight county matches and after getting off to a bad start and losing the first two, they won four of the next six and drew two. They also beat the Indian tourists during that period with Robbie taking five for 18 in their first innings. His participation in the trial was guaranteed as his captaincy skills were growing with every match. His ability to nurse young hopefuls like Denis Compton, who made his debut one week before his eighteenth birthday at the end of June against Sussex, was outstanding. Compton demonstrated that Robbie's faith in him was justified only four days after his debut when he joined his captain at 21 for five in their second innings against Northamptonshire, only 145 runs in front. Together they added 129 runs before Robbie fell for 57: Compton went on to make 87 and Middlesex eventually ran out winners by 283 runs. Other young players blossomed under Robbie's control but there were some who never measured up to his expectations. Ian Peebles later wrote that 'on the field he was alert and forceful, always seeking to keep the game alive, and always ready to take a chance in order to do so. He expected his players to be of the same mind and though patient (to a point) with inept triers, he was fire and brimstone to the slack, selfish or indifferent.' Compton himself occasionally lost his concentration during a long day in the field and would suffer the same tongue-lashing as any other less talented youngster, but even so Peebles would write in 1977: 'Not long ago, Denis said to me that Walter was the best captain he had ever known.'

Despite both Robbie and Holmes being included in the team to represent the South, with Wyatt given the captaincy of the North, Allen was made captain and immediately after the rain-reduced game has ended, he was announced as the new England captain for the First Test against India. Holmes accepted the decision: 'I was not surprised when Gubby Allen was picked as captain in the first Test match against India, and I was omitted from the side altogether. I felt that this was the "writing on the wall" and that, provided he did reasonably well, Gubby would be invited to take the side to Australia.' That forecast would soon prove to be accurate. The decision was unlikely to have surprised Robbie either, as any ambitions he may have had regarding the captaincy for himself would have been discussed privately with Gubby and Warner, and his agreement obtained to wait his turn. Reluctantly perhaps, but the prospect of being given the position of vice-captain for the tour was an attractive alternative.

Robbie played in the First Test at Lord's, which England won comfortably by nine wickets, and also in the Second at Old Trafford which was drawn. He then concentrated on the final weeks of the Championship. Under his command, Middlesex beat Sussex by an innings, beat Gloucestershire by nine wickets, and then drew with Surrey at The Oval. After that, some unexpected demands of his insurance business forced him to take a twelve-day break, but that gave Gubby Allen the opportunity to step in and practice his captaincy skills some more by leading Middlesex to a 192-run win over Hampshire. Robbie stormed back for the last three games, leading Middlesex to victory over Kent by eight wickets, beating Worcestershire by 225 runs, and beating Surrey at Lord's by 256 runs. They finished above Yorkshire as runners-up to the new champions, Derbyshire. Gubby Allen made an enormous contribution in support of his county captain and in his nine appearances took 54 wickets and averaged 50.66 with the bat. They would soon be reversing roles and fighting to recover the Ashes down under.

The England side which drew with India at Old Trafford in July 1936.
Standing (l to r): H.Gimblett, A.E.Fagg, J.Hardstaff, A.R.Gover,
T.S.Worthington, L.B.Fishlock. Seated: H.Verity, R.W.V.Robins,
G.O.B.Allen (capt), W.R.Hammond, G.Duckworth (wk).

Chapter Seven
To Australia with Gubby

At an emergency MCC Committee meeting at Lord's on 20 July 1936, the President informed Gubby Allen, a member of the committee, of his appointment as captain of the MCC team to tour Australia and New Zealand that winter. The press were then notified of the decision and the names of the first six players invited to join the team: Hammond, Leyland, Verity, Hardstaff, Fishlock and Robins. At the beginning of August another four names, Fagg, Copson, Worthington and Duckworth, were added: soon after the selection was completed by the addition of Voce, Barnett, Farnes, Sims, Holmes and confirmation that Ames expected to have recovered from his back problem and would be able to tour. The composition of the touring party was closely examined and became a subject of considerable criticism. The consensus of opinion was that, with no established opening partnership, no off-spinner and several players with little Test experience, the side was one of the weakest ever sent to Australia and that Allen was facing an uphill task. However, some analysts believed that, if Allen could coax and cajole top-class performances from his mixed group of experience and youth, anything might be possible against an Australian team that was itself going through a transitional period after losing several senior players to retirement, and which would probably be playing under the untried leadership of Bradman.

Once the team had been chosen, it would have been customary for the MCC to announce the appointment of a vice-captain. No such announcement was made in the summer of 1936. According to the minutes of a meeting held by the sub-committee at the Carlton Club on Sunday, 9 August, a bizarre decision was made: 'In view of the fact that the appointment of a vice-captain might under certain circumstances introduce difficulties during the progress of the tour, it was decided to make no appointment but to empower the captain to appoint a deputy as circumstances might dictate.' What 'difficulties' they were expecting, who would experience those 'difficulties', and what 'certain circumstances might occur', were not clarified. MCC would not consider any of the professionals as candidates for vice-captain, so the only 'difficulties' that might arise would involve the amateurs, Farnes, Robins and Holmes. Farnes could be ruled out as he was too young and inexperienced to step up into leadership, so we are left with Robbie and Holmes. It seems very likely that Allen, with Warner's approval, may have half-promised Robbie the vice-captaincy, long before he knew that Holmes would be invited to join the tour. The committee, however, may have seen Holmes as a far more suitable choice, bearing in mind that he had already successfully filled that position under Wyatt in the tour of the West Indies in 1934/35, and that as captain of the MCC party in a non-Test tour of Australia and New Zealand the previous winter, had worked hard to restore the old 'pre-Bodyline' relationship and prepare the ground for the full tour in 1936/37.

Was Allen jealous of the reputation that Holmes had already earned in Australia twelve months earlier, so that if he was made vice-captain it might give the impression that the MCC tourists were operating under joint leadership? By not naming either Robbie or Holmes as vice-captain, but giving Allen the exclusive power to appoint a deputy as and when he thought fit, would make it quite clear who was in charge and make certain that neither would feel inferior to the other. But Holmes would have been disappointed that his earlier efforts were not going to be rewarded with at least the vice-captaincy after being passed over as captain, and would probably have suspected that during the tour Allen might favour his friend Robbie as and when he wished. The attempt by the committee to control the situation, prompted by Allen's misgivings, may well have backfired and created the very problems that it had tried to solve. And Robbie would have been caught in the middle of an awkward situation that was not of his making.

But Allen need not have worried. Holmes had to decline the invitation to be part of the touring party, as his father became seriously ill and Holmes, as eldest son, felt that he should be close at hand that winter. The selectors decided that there was no need to replace Holmes as they preferred to keep the size of the touring party to just 16 members. Allen would have none of it and insisted that the original selection of 17 must be maintained, recommending the inclusion of Wyatt as he would bring valuable knowledge and experience. Realising that his inclusion was very much a last-minute choice, Wyatt could be counted on to raise no objections if Robbie acted as vice-captain throughout the tour, as Allen had probably intended from the beginning.

From the moment that *R.M.S.Orion* sailed from Southampton on 12 September, Allen was determined to take control of everything that involved the squad of players under his command. He wanted everyone to know that he was in charge and cultivated the impression of his absolute authority. Unfortunately he was totally unprepared for the pressures that awaited him in Australia.

The first match in Australia was at Perth against Western Australia. In an innings victory, Robbie did not get a turn to bat but had 16 eight-ball overs and took three wickets. That would be his last spell of bowling for a month as later, during some net practice in front of a large crowd, Robbie dived to hold a full-blooded drive from Charlie Barnett and appeared to dislocate a finger in his right hand. Allen revealed in his next letter to his parents on the last day of the match: 'Duckworth dislocated a finger on left and Robbie doing same to top joint of most important finger for bowling on right hand. Former out of cricket probably two weeks, latter three [or] four weeks. However, let's have all our bad luck now. Owing to Robbie's accident must play in next match.' But Robbie's injury was much more serious than a dislocation and Allen was no longer writing about an accident that could be passed off as 'bad luck'. Because it was going to cause him some personal inconvenience, he felt the need to appear the victim of misbehaviour, although he had not been present and therefore not in a position to make such a judgement. Writing in the next letter home he complained: 'Robbie fracturing his most important finger on his right hand, when fooling about at fielding practice, is a disaster.'

Ames was suffering from a recurrence of the back trouble that had kept him from playing most of the summer in England. His condition deteriorated to such an extent that he was talking about returning to Britain on the next boat home. Allen was not prepared to lose such a valuable member of the squad without a fight and sent him in the opposite direction: 'I have packed him off by boat to Melbourne in the care of Robbie to see some doctors.' It also served the purpose of keeping Robbie occupied and having his injured hand re-assessed. Two weeks later the tourists arrived in Melbourne to play Victoria and found Ames making progress towards a full recovery. It was still too early for Robbie to risk playing, so Allen was forced to continue as captain for the match and the one that followed against New South Wales after they had all moved on to Sydney. Even if he had considered placing the team in the hands of Wyatt, it was an option that was denied to him because of yet another injury at the country match at Clare a week earlier, this time to Wyatt, 'breaking a bone in his arm which will keep him out of cricket for at least five or six weeks.'

There were two matches arranged during the two weeks spent in Sydney and MCC suffered their first defeat of the tour to New South Wales. Although Robbie was less than 100% fit, Allen told him to take over the team for the second match which was against an 'Australian XI', while he went off to the seaside for a long weekend, justifying his decision: 'Robbie's finger is better, but I am afraid it is going to be some time before he can bowl properly, but he has restarted in this match as we MUST have him for the first Test.'

Moving on to Brisbane, the next game was against Queensland, the last before the First Test. Allen decided to continue with his break, giving his reasons: 'I decided not to play up here in the State match, as there were so many others who were trying to play into form (in vain, I fear, at present) and have had a good share of it to date.' His share of the bowling in the first five first-class matches had, indeed, been excessive. Seemingly unable to trust his other fast bowlers, he had delivered 89 eight-ball overs himself, twice as many as Farnes, 40 overs, and Copson, also 40 overs, and far more than Voce, 54 overs, despite accusing him of being 'pig fat' in one of his letters and obviously in need of some long spells at the wicket. Robbie had no interest in any self-sacrifice nonsense and in the two games under his captaincy he asked Voce to bowl a total of 55 overs and Farnes 52 overs. This was exactly the workload that they had needed but Allen misunderstood Robbie's motives and had only criticism for his actions during the game against Queensland: 'Robbie has got one of his fits of the funks and simply won't put himself on. If he won't bowl as I told him last night how are we going to find out how he is bowling?' Robbie bowed

*Robbie going out to bat with Maurice Leyland for MCC against
An Australian XI at Sydney Cricket Ground in November 1936.*

to Allen's demands when Queensland needed 500 runs to win on the last
day and he bowled 17 overs, compared with only three in the first innings,
taking four for 63.

The First Test was due to start on 4 December and Allen sat down with his
selection committee of Robins, Wyatt, Leyland and Hammond to pick the
best eleven: 'Choosing the team was not easy, but after much argument
I got the side I wanted. Robbie was splendid and backed me all the way.'
Robbie bowled 17 of England's 85 eight-ball overs in the Australian first
innings, conceding only 48 runs though without a wicket to show for his
efforts. With Australia skittled out for 58 in their second innings England
won by 322 runs.

There was one change to the England team for the Second Test with
Sims being brought in for Worthington after inspections of the wicket
suggested more spin might be required and the damage to Robbie's hand
still restricted his ability to bowl using his normal grip and delivery for
any length of time. In the event, Robbie was only required to bowl eight
overs in the match and wasn't needed to bat. Allen won the toss again and
by the start of the third day England were 426-6 with Hammond not out
231. Before play commenced there had been heavy rain and Allen decided
it was not the right time to continue batting and immediately declared. By
2.30 pm Australia were all out for 80 after only 24 overs with Voce and
Allen taking seven of the wickets between them. With the wicket showing
definite signs of improvement, Allen had to make a choice between asking
Australia to follow on 346 runs behind, or bat again and hope to score

another 200 or more to make the England position impregnable. With rain about, Allen opted to put the Australians straight back in, but things didn't go the way Allen had expected, so that by the end of the day Australia had reduced England's lead to 201 for the loss of only one wicket with Bradman well set at 57 not out.

During that dramatic third day there had been an incident involving Robbie and a brief exchange of words with Allen, the contents of which have been discussed at length over the years and created a myth frequently included within books and articles covering the history of the Ashes.

The facts seem to be these. Australia lost their first wicket after following on at 38 for one and were slowly reducing England's huge lead with difficulty when, according to the following day's *Sydney Morning Herald*, 'HOT CHANCE. Bradman at 24 made a fierce hook shot off Allen, and Robins, at square-leg, missed the most difficult of chances, the ball failing to stick in his right hand.' Elsewhere on the same page in the newspaper an in-depth report commented: 'Bradman made a vigorous shot off Allen and the ball travelled with great pace towards Robins, fielding near the square-leg umpire. Robins got the ball in his damaged right hand, but he could not hold it.' *The Age* newspaper reported on the same day: 'When Bradman had made 24 he hooked a ball from Allen vigorously and gave Robins a smoking-hot chance at square leg.'

That evening Allen wrote to his father: 'We would have been in an impregnable position tonight if Robins had caught Don Bradman about 4.50 this afternoon off me for 24 at short leg. It was a 'sitter' and I have got a horrible sinking feeling inside me that it may cost us the match.' So the 'most difficult of chances' or 'smoking-hot chance' had suddenly become a 'sitter' in Allen's eyes. Neither *Wisden* in its report of the match, nor Cardus in his book about the tour, made any reference to a catch being dropped. As it turned out, the 'catch' made no difference to the result as Australia collapsed after the dismissal of Fingleton for 73, Bradman at 82, and McCabe at 93, and were all out for 324, giving England an innings victory. Even so, six days later, Allen was, incredibly, still complaining that the doubts over his decision to make Australia follow on would never have been raised: 'if Robbie had caught Bradman off me when he had made 24, as he most certainly ought to have done.' Fifty years later the reasons for Allen's attitude were revealed in *Wisden Cricket Monthly* when John Arlott reported that when Robbie went to Allen to offer his genuine, but perhaps unnecessary, apology for not being able to hold the catch, he received the sarcastic reply: 'Don't give it a thought, Walter, it has probably cost us the rubber but don't give it a thought.' In his 'authorised' biography of Allen, published two years later, Swanton had heard a different version and wrote that Robins, 'the man who scarcely ever dropped a catch, floored one which was going hard but straight at his throat', apologised to Allen, who responded: 'Oh, forget it, old boy, it's probably cost us the rubber, but what the hell!' Swanton then tried to play the situation down by justifying Allen's unfair criticism by giving him the chance to explain: 'Robbie was such a temperamental chap I thought the best thing was to try and make him laugh.' It doesn't sound any funnier 80 years later but Swanton went even further to try and excuse the comment by saying that Robbie himself had found the exchange amusing: 'In later years at least, the culprit did laugh about it, long and often.' Neither of the two sons of the so-called 'culprit' can remember Robbie ever recounting the circumstances with the same good humour that he recalled many other events during his long and varied career.

In a letter written on Christmas Eve to Gubby's father, Robbie seems anxious to reassure a worried parent by saying: 'We have blended ourselves into a team and Gubby has been magnificent,' and then later, 'Gubby is in great form and as fit as a fiddle.' Little did Robbie know that his friend was about to enter a period where the pressures of leadership would seriously affect his ability to keep his emotions under control.

The Third Test started on New Year's Day in Melbourne with England holding Australia to 181 for six on the first day, although the dismissal of Bradman for only 13 was an embarrassment for Allen, according to Bradman during an interview in *Wisden Cricket Monthly* in 1983. As Verity ran in to bowl, Robbie suddenly realised that, positioned alongside the square-leg umpire, he was not where Allen had wanted him to be and he swiftly moved ten yards closer to the batsman. Bradman said that he had memorised all the field placings just before Verity began his run and when the ball arrived he turned it off his thigh without attempting to deflect it downwards, because he believed there were no fieldsmen nearby. Robbie took the catch; there is nothing in the Laws of Cricket to say that he shouldn't, although it had generally been understood that, apart from advancing a few steps towards the batsman as the bowler runs in, fieldsmen should not change their position. At close of play Bradman remonstrated with Robbie over the incident and received such sincere and profound apologies that he invited Robbie to stay for the week-end at his home in Adelaide during the Fourth Test to develop their growing friendship further. (It might be thought that their relationship derived from Bradman's masonic affiliations; Robbie though was never a freemason. Their friendship seems to have developed through a shared interest in the techniques and technicalities of cricket.)

Heavy overnight rain delayed the start of play on the second day until after lunch. The Australian innings lasted little more than another half-hour when Bradman declared at 200 for nine, putting England in to bat at 3 pm on one of Melbourne's notorious sticky wickets. Cardus wrote: 'I could scarcely believe my eyesight as I saw the ball's preposterous behaviour. It described all manner of angles and curves: it was here, there, everywhere, spitting, darting, fizzing.' When the follow-on had been saved, both Robbie and Wyatt advised declaration with more than an hour of playing time available and an opportunity to take advantage of the horrendous conditions and grab several Australian second-innings wickets, even if Bradman reversed his batting order and sacrificed the tail-enders. When Hammond was out at 69 for four Robbie was on his knees imploring Allen to declare but Allen dithered and lost five more wickets for the addition of a paltry eight runs. Wasting nine precious minutes without scoring, Allen stormed off, finally declaring at 76 for nine, but with only about 30 minutes left for play in deteriorating light. Cardus was not optimistic: 'It seemed a grim belated joke, as well as strategy hopeful and embarrassed and enforced.' O'Reilly went first ball but fewer than three overs were bowled before Fleetwood-Smith and Ward succeeded in convincing the umpires, after several appeals against the bad light, that it was time to end play for the day.

By Monday afternoon, after several interruptions the wicket had started to calm down and Bradman and Fingleton saw Australia safely to 194 for five by the end of the day. Eventually, they added 346 for the sixth wicket and England needed 689 runs to win. To their credit, England never gave up trying, although it seemed all over when Robbie joined Leyland at 195 for six. Going on the attack from the start, Robbie drove his first ball through the covers and they ran two before he turned for a third, but Leyland waved him back: 'Steady lad, you know we can't get 'em all tonight!' Next day they added 86 runs in 45 minutes before Robbie was bowled by O'Reilly for 61, his innings described by Cardus as 'gay, impudent dartings up and down were like a sort of whimsical dance of death in England's extreme hour.' After his departure at 306 for seven the England innings soon ended with the addition of only 17 more runs.

By now Allen's letters home were containing longer passages of complaint about the pressures he was under, and how his health and mental stability were being worn down by the demands being put upon him, on and off the field. There was a three-week break between the Third and Fourth Test in which MCC would have to travel to Tasmania for two first-class matches. Licking his wounds, Allen decided to stay over in Melbourne for the first week to mix pleasure with some personal business meetings. Wyatt was going to make his return to action at last and Robbie welcomed him back into the team for an innings victory over Tasmania, during which Robbie took two important wickets and gave himself the heaviest bowling load of 18 overs. Allen flew over to Launceston in time to lead the team in a draw with a Combined XI. He then wrote a long letter to his father in which he launched an extraordinary series of complaints about Robbie:

> The one real disappointment on the trip in many ways, but this is between you and me only, is Robbie. He is very difficult on occasions when he should be setting a good example and is now going through one of his spasms of saying he hates cricket, is no good at it, and wants to go home. It is essential that he plays in the Tests but at the present moment he simply can't bowl at all and looks as though he isn't trying. He will never go on another tour, I know, and on the whole I think it is a good thing. I am very fond of him still and he amuses me a great deal but he has done some unwise things and the pros don't respect him anymore. He thinks it is clever to defy authority and refuses to see that it is a hopeless view to take especially on tour.

Allen seemed to have forgotten that Robbie had just spent nearly three months frustrated by the serious damage to his hand which had prevented him from bowling in any way close to the standard he usually reached. Nor does he acknowledge that only four weeks after receiving that injury he had expected Robbie to play and had entrusted him with the leadership for two consecutive first-class matches in November and then discovered afterwards that, following a series of disjointed performances from most of the players under his own captaincy, the whole side now simply refused to be downhearted and the tide had turned. Allen also conveniently forgot to mention that when it suited him to take a week off to enjoy himself with friends and family in Sydney between the First and Second Tests, and then another week off later in Melbourne before rejoining the team in Tasmania, he had no problem handing the leadership over to Robbie on each occasion. It also doesn't seem to have occurred to Allen that over the past two months Robbie had not missed a day's play from any of the ten matches played, including three Tests, and that before he arrived in Tasmania, the last time Allen saw Robbie playing was during the Third Test at Melbourne where the Australian press reported 'squeals of delight from the female spectators in the 87,000 crowd as Robins ran, swooped, gathered and threw in a spectacular fashion that hadn't been seen on a cricket field before', hardly the actions of someone who, according to Allen 'looks as though he isn't trying'.

There is no doubt that Robbie could rub people up the wrong way with his own particular brand of humour. He was a notorious leg-puller. He enjoyed poking fun at authority. To have 'defied authority' as Allen claims, sounds much more serious, but there is no other record, official or unofficial, of him having done so during the tour. It is difficult to imagine that the zealous, fervent and confident Robbie would ever declare that he 'hates cricket, is no good at it, and wants to go home'. Presumably he was hugely frustrated by his inability to bowl to his own high standards because of the time it was taking to recover from the effects of the hand injury. It seems that either Allen had misread the situation or Robbie had exaggerated his feelings in a one-off outburst, because the depression, if that is what it was and not an elaborate wind-up, was short-lived and Robbie would be back playing as enthusiastically as ever in the next six matches.

England made two changes for the next Test by replacing Worthington with Farnes and bringing in Wyatt for Sims. By reducing the number of spin-bowlers in the side meant that many more overs would probably be required from Robbie, which seems a strange decision at odds with Allen's grumbles ten days earlier. England started well and had a first innings lead of 42 runs but then Bradman came in to his own with another double century and the final target of 392 runs proved too much for the England.

Allen decided to miss the two games at Geelong, preferring to stay in Melbourne visiting friends and family, even though injuries meant that Robbie did not have a full eleven to lead and the MCC tour manager, Rupert Howard, had to be drafted into the side. The visit to the capital, Canberra, and the various official receptions planned for them there meant that Allen had to be present, even though he decided not to actually play against the Southern Districts of New South Wales XI and asked Wyatt to take over the team, giving Robbie a well-deserved rest at last. Allen left Canberra as soon as he had performed the duties expected of him and stayed with friends for the weekend, deciding to skip the match in Sydney against New South Wales, re-instating Robbie as captain. He eventually drove to Sydney and arrived while the match was in progress, but reacted badly to more demands on his time, official and unofficial. A meeting with Robbie, Howard and Wyatt convinced him that he should leave at once and extend his holiday from affairs of cricket even further, including the next game against Victoria in Melbourne. So once again, Robbie continued as leader of the squad, a responsibility to which he was now well accustomed despite Allen's reservations about his commitment. Since 17 November Allen had only played in two state games out of seven and had missed three out of four of the two-day country matches.

Allen rejoined the team in Melbourne three days before the final Test. He was disturbed to hear that, during the match against Victoria, the fast bowler Nash had upset MCC batsmen with a stream of bouncers and that the Australian selectors had included Nash in their list of 13 names for the Test. The Australians also included McCormick, another fast bowler inclined to use bouncers as a regular part of his attack. Taking Robbie with him as a witness to the discussion, he met Bradman over lunch and told him that if the selection of both fast bowlers meant an onslaught of short-pitched deliveries, England would feel free to retaliate. Bradman resented this interference in his choice of players, but Robbie was able to influence both captains into realising that they needed to draw back from what could develop into an awkward stand-off with neither prepared to back down. It was agreed that the occasional bouncer at batsmen on either side would be acceptable.

This would be Robbie's last involvement with the tour in any capacity. In choosing the team for the final Test, Allen had decided to rely entirely on the opinions of the other selectors based on current form during the past two state matches while he was elsewhere. Allen did not like going into the match without a leg-spinner but his argument, damning Robbie with faint praise, 'even if he is bad he produces variation', was not strong enough to convince the others to keep Robbie in the side.

Whatever he felt privately about the decision to drop him, Robbie knew what to do next. Seven months earlier at Lord's, the MCC Committee had agreed that there would be no objection to Robbie returning to England at the conclusion of the Australian portion of the tour, should business commitments demand his personal attention. Robbie stayed just long enough to watch the start of the Test and wish the team good luck before going off to accept an invitation to go shooting in South Australia, an exercise designed to help strengthen his damaged finger. Eventually England lost and the victorious Australian captain then invited Robbie to stay with him and his wife Jessie at their home in Adelaide until there was a ship available to take him back to England. They competed with each other at golf and various other sports, with Robbie usually the winner, but when he had added billiards to his repertoire of superiority, his host had had enough. Bradman invited a friend to dinner but when he was introduced as Walter Lindrum, Robbie did not recognise the name as that of the current world billiards champion. Challenged to a game, Robbie found himself outclassed before the penny dropped and Bradman confessed to his subterfuge. Soon after it was time for Robbie to fly from Adelaide to Perth and board his ship for its voyage home.

Allen was in two minds about the departure of his friend: 'Robbie has gone home in the *Orion* and, though he did worry me to death, I shall miss him terribly as he always has something funny to say.' This did not prevent him from putting Robbie first on his list of disappointments when assessing performances after the tour was over: 'The following list of complete failures speaks for itself — Robins, Worthington, Fagg, Fishlock, Sims, Wyatt (through injury) and Hardstaff (in Tests).' It seems unfair that he would qualify Wyatt's inclusion as being as a result of injury, but does not extend the same excuse to Robbie, and that he fails to give Robbie any credit for the enormous debt he owed him for standing in for him so frequently, when he personally felt he needed rest and recuperation, and ignored the fact that Robbie himself could have benefited from the same consideration. Talking to Anthony Meredith fifty years later, Allen paused for thought when asked who had been his greatest helper on the tour, and the author picked up on his hesitation and wrote: 'The captaincy, it seemed, had been a lonely job,' before Allen gave his limited list: 'I had two or three quite intelligent chaps. Robbie. Robbie was intelligent, when he was paying attention. Bob Wyatt, of course. Maurice Leyland.' Reluctantly perhaps, but proof that Allen had always valued the part played by Robbie in Australia, even if he could never bring himself to admit it at the time.

Chapter Eight
Captain of England

Robbie was back in England in time to play in the first match of the 1937 season at Lord's. Gubby Allen had not yet returned from California so the captaincy of MCC's side against Yorkshire was given to Wyatt. Allen had made it very clear that he would not be available to continue as the England captain that summer, as he did not intend to play very much first-class cricket.

Robbie's record in the first weeks of the season leading Middlesex had been a roller-coaster ride between success and failure. But that was about to end when Yorkshire returned to Lord's for the county match. Robbie top-scored with an unbeaten 65 in Middlesex's only innings and inspired his bowlers to win by an innings. This was the sort of leadership that the selectors were looking for and the next Middlesex match was as hosts to the New Zealand tourists. Robbie's five for 42 in the visitors' second innings convinced Warner and Co that he was the right captain for England and his stint began with the First Test at Lord's on 26 June where his chosen eleven was a mixture of old friends and new. Six members of the tour down under, Barnett, Hardstaff, Hammond, Ames, Voce and Verity, plus one player who should have been with them on that tour, Paynter, two debutants, Hutton and Parks, and Gover, the best fast bowler they could find to replace the missing Allen.

Winning the toss seemed like a good omen for Robbie's future as England's new skipper but when they lost their first two wickets for only 31, some might have had doubts. A partnership of 245 between Hammond and Hardstaff brought England back on track to a first innings total of 424, and they soon had New Zealand struggling at 176 for seven with Robbie leading by example with three for 58. But he couldn't break a century partnership between Maloney and Roberts and England had to be satisfied with a lead of 129. As always, Robbie believed that victory was possible and sent himself in at the fall of the fourth wicket, 292 in front, to hurry the score along. Eventually he declared at lunch on the last day 355 in front with four hours in which to get all ten New Zealand wickets. He very nearly pulled it off and when the match ended New Zealand were 175 for eight.

Robbie's luck with the coin continued in the Second Test and England ended the first day at 358 for nine. He declared first thing on Monday morning and at 119 for five the New Zealanders were again in difficulties. But Robbie could take no further part in the bowling attack after dislocating the index finger of his right hand trying to take a hard chance off Goddard, and then shortly afterwards he split the third finger of the same hand when stopping a hard cut, and New Zealand escaped having to follow on. Then it was England's turn to collapse and at 75 for seven their slender lead of 152 looked vulnerable on the last day. But fielding mistakes allowed the last three wickets to add 112 runs after they had been encouraged by Robbie to attack the bowling to give his own bowlers enough time to bowl New Zealand out, no matter how slim the lead. Disheartened at the change from looking potential winners to fighting to save the match, New Zealand lost their last six wickets for 40 runs.

The final Test was at The Oval and once again Robbie's positive attitude in search of another win might have paid off if there had been more than only half-an-hour's play on the first day. New Zealand progressed steadily on the second day and when Page had reached his half-century Robbie put himself on to bowl and took the last three wickets for the addition of only another five more runs. At the end of play England had raced to 86 for three but as soon as they had passed New Zealand's first innings of 249 for the loss of only seven wickets on the third day, Robbie declared. Ringing the changes between seven bowlers, including Hutton and Compton, he hoped to skittle New Zealand out for a total low enough that England could reach before the drawing of stumps. Given enough time England, with the talents of Hutton, Hardstaff, Hammond and the debutant Compton, who had made 65 in the first innings, the eventual target of 183 would probably have been within their reach, but the match ended with England 31 for one after ten overs.

Robbie's tactics throughout the series did not impress everyone and in Warner's opinion, 'Robins had captained well and his fielding was inspiring, but he was more of a battle-cruiser or destroyer leader than an Admiral of the Fleet. He was always out for the "kill" but, as has been suggested, he perhaps attempted to "kill" before he was really in a position to do so.' So it seems that, in the mind of the chairman of the selectors at least, there was a question mark over whether Robbie should retain the captaincy when the Australians arrived next summer. There would be no MCC winter tour and without another Test series on which to judge the merits of whoever might have been chosen as captain, any decision would have to be put on hold for another seven months.

* * * * * * *

As well as his success as the new England captain, inspiring his players to play aggressive, entertaining cricket as the best way to win matches, Robbie was driving his Middlesex team to even greater efforts in his determination to be the top county. He had a small squad of experienced players but there were younger players showing great promise and Robbie believed that time and money should be spent on the provision of better playing facilities in the cities and rural areas, so that even more would emerge to strengthen English cricket. Immediately after his return from Australia he had written to *The Cricketer* magazine:

> During the recent MCC Australian tour nothing impressed me so much as the contrast between the concrete wickets on which the young Australian learns the game and the so-called turf wickets in our parks

and many of our village greens with which the young Englishman is forced to contend. Both in the big cities of Australia (just outside the famous Sydney ground there are about 30 of these concrete wickets) and in the most remote parts up-country these concrete wickets are to be found, some in the roughest of fields, some amidst scrub inches high, and others on plains absolutely devoid of grass or any other vegetation.

He urged that the various playing field authorities should give the matter their earnest and immediate consideration because 'the average young Australian cricketer of today is streets ahead of the average young Englishman, and the main reason for this is, in my humble opinion, the concrete wicket.'

The Middlesex committee needed to find a suitable deputy when county fixtures clashed with Robbie's international duties. John Human was prepared to make himself available only occasionally, but Middlesex were lucky to find that W.H. 'Tagge' Webster was also willing to step up when necessary. Webster had followed the same path as Robbie from Highgate School to Cambridge University and even into the Corinthians, where he had sometimes played alongside Robbie, and then into the Middlesex team under him, so he knew what was expected from him as captain.

Middlesex started badly with just one win in May from four games while Yorkshire streaked ahead with three wins from five matches. The day after Middlesex had lost to Lancashire in early June, Yorkshire arrived in St John's Wood ready to put an end to the Middlesex challenge for the title before it had barely got off the ground. Robbie and his team had other ideas. Dismissing the current champions for 218, Middlesex had built a small lead when Robbie came in at 283 for six and he increased that lead to 153 by ending unbeaten with 65 scored out of the last 88 runs of the innings. Thanks to some great spin bowling from Sims, five for 36, Yorkshire crumbled to an innings defeat. But despite this significant victory, Middlesex made only a marginal improvement in June with three wins and two losses. Yorkshire on the other hand were unfazed by their loss to their rivals and won five of their eight matches that month. In July Middlesex won six of their seven games and, most important of all, took five points from their draw at Sheffield when Yorkshire had been looking for revenge. Yorkshire could only manage four wins from their eight games and so, after the leadership had changed hands four times during the month, Middlesex finally leapfrogged over them to the top of the table, helped along at one stage by Robbie's second hat-trick, against Somerset at Lord's.

The last championship games were due to begin on 28 August. After Yorkshire had won four of their last five games and Middlesex had won five out of their last six, both counties were down to their last two matches. Because counties played a different total of matches the title would be decided on percentages and with Middlesex now having 238 points with a percentage of 72.12, and Yorkshire 271 points with a percentage of 69.74, it meant that if Middlesex won both of their last matches it would not be possible for Yorkshire to overtake them. Some critics felt that winning the title by playing four fewer matches was unfair. Robbie did not take kindly to that criticism and, believing that his team was superior was prepared to prove it in a one-off challenge. He sent a telegram to Brian Sellers, the Yorkshire captain, suggesting a match in September to decide which was the better team, whatever the points and percentages in the final championship table might say. Sellers agreed and offered to make it even more interesting by suggesting a wager of £10 per man, to which Robbie immediately agreed but the Yorkshire committee over-ruled Sellers and all bets were off, officially at any rate.

But before it was clear which official champion was being challenged by which official runner-up, there were the two more county matches to be played. Middlesex could only draw at Trent Bridge and the next day faced Surrey at Lord's, knowing that as Yorkshire had beaten Sussex, only a win would bring them the title. Three weeks earlier Middlesex had won at The Oval but in this rematch Surrey were not prepared to lie down and be the sacrificial lambs while Middlesex celebrated their coronation. Surrey batted first and their 509 seemed to have put the match beyond the title-contenders. It was during the Surrey run-fest that Robbie gave signs that he was finally feeling the strain of what had been a demanding season. He was bowling his leg-spinners but was not having a very good day and at the end of an over Bill Reeves the umpire, who had just rejected two loud appeals, turned to him and asked 'Would you like your sweater, sir?' holding out the official Middlesex sweater bearing the three scimitars. Robins snapped 'No, you can stick it right up your ... .' Bill swiftly replied 'What, swords an' all?' Things got worse when Middlesex began their reply by losing their first two wickets for only four runs. Enter Patsy Hendren playing in his last match at Lord's at the age of 48. He was greeted by a battery of photographers, a tremendous ovation from the crowd. With Edrich as his partner they added 182 runs for the third wicket and he went on to reach his century at which moment everyone in the ground stood up and sang 'For he's a jolly good fellow.' Middlesex ended only 90 runs behind and but then Surrey rushed to a lead of 294 before declaring with about three hours left for play. Robbie told Holmes, the Surrey captain, that his team would go for the runs 'regardless', as a draw would not be enough. Patsy went for a duck in his very last innings but Gubby Allen had answered the call to arms to help Robbie in this important match and anything seemed possible when Robbie went out to the middle to join him at 158 for seven. They added another 24 runs before, with fifteen minutes left for play, Holmes made his last gamble for victory. He put himself on to bowl and tossed four deliveries high and wide of the wicket with instructions to the fielders not to prevent the ball reaching the boundary. With this tactic he ensured that the Middlesex total passed 200 runs and he was entitled to take the new ball and attempt to grab the last three wickets with his pace bowlers. Gubby was furious and demanded that the umpires did something about what he considered a blatant abuse of the Laws. When he was told that there was nothing they could do, he disagreed and appealed against light, despite the fact that the sun was still shining

Robbie escorting Pat Hendren onto the field of play from the professionals'
entrance at the start of his last match for Middlesex at Lord's
on 28 August 1937.

brightly. To avoid further argument the umpires upheld the appeal and took the players off the field to end play for the day.

Yorkshire had beaten Hampshire at Bournemouth so the final table confirmed that they were champions once again. A neutral ground had been agreed for the challenge match and on 11 September the match began at the Kennington Oval with Yorkshire at full strength but Middlesex without Compton, who was playing football for Arsenal. The match was scheduled for four days to ensure a result and, despite ending on the third day, raised over £700 for various charities. Yorkshire won the toss and at close of play on the Saturday were 293 for six. They went on to 401 on the Monday but Middlesex, caught on a turning wicket, ended the day at 63 for six. Things went from bad to worse for Middlesex who followed on 216 runs behind and were then dismissed for 101 on the Tuesday, with Verity taking eight for 43 to give him match figures of ten for 94, and lost by an innings. The Yorkshire members of the crowd celebrated their victory with some good-natured singing, in particular several renditions of 'Who killed Cock Robin?', directed at Robbie by those who mistook his indefatigable confidence as nothing more than 'cockiness'.

But apart from all the county cricket and Test match drama of that exciting summer with Robbie playing the leading man, another member of the Robins family was quietly making a unique contribution to the world of cricket. Uncle Vernon was still captain at East Molesey Cricket Club and working behind the scenes to ensure that everything ran like clockwork for players, members and visitors. But his new project was the construction of the most comprehensive scoreboard in the country. He began by designing and putting the pieces together in the attic of his home at Kingston Hill, but as it grew in size he moved everything down into his back garden, where it was eventually completed and erected ready for transportation to the ground.

Chapter Nine

Disappointment

Robbie looked forward to another opportunity to overtake Yorkshire in the 1938 season with a Middlesex team full of young players about to realise their potential. But with the Australians arriving for a series of five Tests, he realised that he may have to play a part-time role as county skipper as he expected the England selectors to ask him to continue as captain of England. That dream was about to be jeopardised by the announcement that Gubby Allen had decided to make a comeback playing first-class cricket that summer and, once he had proved that he was fully fit, apparently expected to be re-instated as England's captain.

Robbie was encouraged to believe that he was the front-runner for the England appointment when he was asked to captain MCC against Surrey in the opening match of the season at Lord's. This was followed by leading Middlesex to two successive championship victories. Gubby had not yet started playing and with the Australian tourists expected next at Lord's to play their traditional match against MCC, Warner and the other selectors were anxious that he should lead the side so that they could assess his fitness. Their request was refused and according to Jim Swanton: 'Gubby, who was at the meeting, said he was not prepared to expose himself this early. A fairly heated discussion followed and Plum was upset by his declining, to put it mildly.' The selectors turned to Robbie again, who was delighted at the opportunity to revive his friendship with Bradman.

Middlesex lost their next game, to Lancashire, and then Gubby Allen rode in with all guns blazing to revive the county's fortunes by playing a major role in an innings victory over Nottinghamshire, followed by another over Worcestershire, contributing 64 and 53 and ten wickets from 47 overs. He was due to play next day for Middlesex against the Australians, but his back trouble had returned and he cried off. That weekend the selectors announced the teams for the trial match at Lord's on the following Wednesday and named Hammond as captain of an 'England XI' and Allen as the captain of a 'Rest of England XI'. At the start of the season Hammond had said that he would in future be playing as an amateur and had just acquired some necessary captaincy experience by taking over as captain of Gloucestershire in their last two county matches. This development had excited Warner, who saw Hammond as potentially an ideal captain of the England Test team. Robbie's omission from either side in the trial came as a shock, but the final decision concerning the Test series had yet to be made. Allen had assumed that he was still the obvious choice and he resented the trial selection, according to Swanton: 'Gubby was angry that the captain's roles were not reversed. In the event he declined, saying he was not fit, and did not again appear in first-class cricket until July. He was upset, not only by the decision, but by the fact that Warner had given him no prior notice of it.' Warner hadn't spoken to Robbie either, but at no time does Swanton make any reference to Robbie's more legitimate claim to the position of captain, or that Allen was prepared to push him aside.

In the meantime, Robbie got on with the job in hand, trying to lead his Middlesex team to victory over the Australians. Rain ruled out any play on the first day but then the match had a sensational start with the visitors all out for 132. Middlesex collapsed to 92 for five but then Robbie joined Compton and they added 68 runs, 43 of them from the captain on the counter-attack. The Australian were 56 runs behind when they started their second innings on the last day but there was not enough time for either side to win the match. However, there was time for someone to add his name to the record books, thanks to Robbie and Bradman putting their heads together during the tea interval. Edrich needed only another ten runs to have completed 1,000 runs during the month of May, not achieved since Hallows did it in 1928. Instead of batting on to close of play, Robbie asked Bradman to declare when they cleared the arrears and added enough runs to prevent Middlesex from going for a win, leaving Edrich time to open the batting and score the runs he needed. At 5.09 pm Bradman did as he had been asked and ended his team's second innings at 114 for two, giving Middlesex just six overs to make 59. Edrich only needed eleven minutes to reach his milestone and Middlesex ended at 21 for no wicket. The Test Trial proceeded as arranged, with Wilcox of Essex taking the place of Allen, and immediately after, when Hammond was confirmed as the new England captain, Robbie confided to Kathleen that being passed over was easily the biggest disappointment of his life.

During the month of May Middlesex had won four of their five county matches and were top of the table, well in front of Yorkshire, who had only won two of their five and been overtaken by Lancashire. As the counties continued to play an unequal number of games and Yorkshire had increased their programme to 30 matches with Middlesex still at 24, the championship title was now calculated on an average 'points per match' basis. Determined to demonstrate that, whether England's captain or not, he was the best allrounder available, Robbie hit 137 against Sussex at Lord's, his highest championship score, and then took six for 69 forcing Sussex to follow on. It was during this match that he learned that Dr Johnston had passed away on 5 June, two years after retiring as head of Highgate School. Always interested in ballistics, Johnston had just completed a series of articles being published in *The Cricketer* under the title 'The Revolutions of a Cricket Ball and Their Revelations' in which he explained, on mathematical principles, the mysteries of 'spin' and 'swerve'. Kathleen recalls that 'a great deal of this was written at our home at Burnham, Bucks, usually at night after dinner. Following one or two mishaps with the cricket ball, they resorted to oranges, and the talk with an occasional thump would go on well after Mrs Johnston and I had retired.'

In the next match, against Hampshire, Robbie took seven for 77 in their second innings to ensure another Middlesex victory, but the England selectors even passed him over for the place as leg spinner and preferred to choose Doug Wright of Kent for the First Test. Another disappointment followed at Leeds in a match that only lasted two days and where both counties were without key players away on Test duty at Trent Bridge, Edrich and Compton from Middlesex and Hutton and Verity for Yorkshire. Middlesex were all out for 105, but with Robbie taking four for 24, they kept the Yorkshire lead to only 68. Middlesex managed to reach only 148 in their second innings and Yorkshire finished winners by seven wickets. Even so, after Middlesex had won two of their next three matches and Yorkshire remained unbeaten in the month of June, Middlesex were still in front with 96 points giving them an average of 7.27, while Yorkshire had an average of 7.17 from their 120 points. Middlesex made a poor start to July drawing their first two matches before Robbie asked Peebles to come to Trent Bridge where Middlesex needed a good result over Nottinghamshire if they were to stay in the race for the title. The pitch had a bit of bounce and pace, Peebles took seven wickets and Middlesex grabbed a win at the last minute. He would stay in the side for the rest of the season, apart from one match, and later wrote: 'These were some of the happiest days of my active cricket life. I was back with old friends and doing quite well.'

Then Yorkshire came to Lord's and, as in the previous season, with so much riding on the result, Middlesex rose to the occasion. Robbie won the toss and sent Yorkshire in to bat on a rain-affected wicket. The ball flew dangerously from the start and Hutton suffered a broken finger, Leyland a broken thumb, and Gibb could take no further part in the match after being hit on the head. Robbie sportingly allowed Yorkshire to bring in Wood to play as substitute wicketkeeper for Gibb throughout both Middlesex innings, although they still batted three short in their second innings and Middlesex won by eight wickets. Unfortunately this was followed by losing to Kent at Maidstone, despite Robbie's brave 83 out of the first-innings total of 159, trying again to make up for the absence of Compton and Edrich playing in the Fourth Test, and with only three wins in six matches in July, Middlesex dropped to second place. They could win only three out of seven in August and failed to match the final run-in from Yorkshire who were unbeaten that month and took the title again.

Regrettably, we shall never know what would have happened if Robbie had been retained as England captain. The whole Ashes series could have been turned on its head if he had been there in the First Test to make one of his usual positive decisions and declared England's first innings closed at 487 for five, after Compton was out, and given his bowlers ten overs before lunch on the second day, instead of waiting until the middle of the afternoon, as Hammond did, to declare at 658 for eight, with the match safe but a result unlikely. At least Robbie and Bradman had a chance to discuss what 'might-have-been' that summer when the series was over and Don and Jessie came to stay with the Robins family for a fortnight at their home in Burnham Beeches, while Don recuperated from the ankle injury he suffered during the Fifth Test at The Oval. Kathleen remembered that when he broke his ankle in that disastrous Test at The Oval, he came down to be nursed with doctors, masseuse and secretaries coming down from London daily to minister to him. He really was quite a prima donna, but very easy to provide for. Rice crispies for breakfast and buttered toast for tea, otherwise I don't think he noticed what he was eating. He was writing an article for 'Wisden's Cricket at the Crossroads'. Don stayed with us until Jessie arrived from Australia and then the four of us had a very gay time until they sailed away for home!

It wasn't long before Bradman had got back onto his feet and, with the Burnham Beeches Golf Club almost literally on the doorstep, he and Robbie began a series of highly contested matches to aid his complete recovery. There is a well-aired story within the Robins family recalled by Charles Robins that they

were evenly matched as RWV by then had had plenty of opportunity to practice and reduced his handicap down to four. On this occasion, in the midst of a very tight contest, while playing the twelfth hole, which is a par 4 but with a blind second shot to a sunken green, RWV said to Don after he had driven down the fairway 'you need a 4 or 5 iron, and play on that prominent tree which can be seen at the back of the green' Don was not happy at this and went to the edge of the hill to gauge the shot for himself, took out the chosen club and put the rest down as an additional mark of the line. Very unusually he then topped the ball, which proceeded to ricochet into his clubs at the top of the hill. 'I suppose you're going to claim the hole?' said Don. To which RWV replied 'well, depends whether we are playing the rules of golf.' Don picked up his ball and walked to the next tee and the rest of the round was played in total silence. Of course, they made it up, and RWV said afterwards that if Don had not remained silent he would never have enforced the rule, but it was too good an opportunity to miss!

Jessie and Don Bradman, Kathleen Robins and Robbie on the golf course at Burnham Beeches, in 1938. Matches between Robbie and the Don could be very competitive.

It seems that Gubby Allen was never able to come to terms with the friendship between Robbie and Don Bradman, which would grow stronger over the next 30 years, and made no attempt to hide his attempts to replace Robbie as Bradman's confidante. Writing to Robbie from Australia during the 1953/54 Ashes series Gubby complained: 'I have seen Sir Donald 3 or 4 times but despite my efforts to have a friendly talk I haven't got to first base and I propose to retire from the unequal contest.' Back in Australia seven years later, Gubby was still at a loss to understand why Bradman showed no interest in building a stronger relationship between them and wrote to Robbie: 'I played golf with Don on the Sunday of the First Test but otherwise have hardly seen him. Don spoke for 41 minutes at the Board of Control dinner. I do not think he likes me much as, though an opposing captain on the very ground on which he was speaking, I got no mention.'

At the beginning of January 1939, Robbie resigned the Middlesex captaincy due to pressures of business. Ian Peebles was approached to see if he would play for the whole of 1939 and captain the side: 'When invited by the Committee to succeed Walter, I was very conscious of the fact that I was taking over from probably the best reigning county captain in England.' Under Peebles, Middlesex had another successful season, winning 14 and losing six matches, once again finishing runners-up to Yorkshire. In the last match of the season Peebles was unable to play at Lord's against Somerset, so Robbie stepped up to take over as captain, only his fourth match that year; he led them to victory after hitting 84 in the Middlesex second innings.

Any plans he may have had for a full return to first-class cricket in the 1940 season were about to be put on hold by the dramatic events unfolding on the world stage.

Chapter Ten
The War Years

On 3 September 1939, the British Prime Minister, Neville Chamberlain, announced that Britain was at war with Germany and Kathleen recorded in her memoir:

> Immediately war was declared, all the young men rushed to get in the Forces. The Territorials had already been called. I remember Ian Peebles and Jim Swanton coming to stay with us on their way to join their respective units, both in uniform. Many of Walter's cricketing pals went into the Army; Walter's brother, Vernon, a regular soldier and married to a general's daughter, might have seen him enrolled into his Regiment, but Walter had no experience at all of soldiering, even less of sailing. He fancied the R.A.F. Eventually Walter got his call-up and was drafted to Uxbridge as Pilot Officer P.T. This did not please him greatly, but at least he was near enough to get home from time to time. As everyone knows, the summer of 1940 was grim and we were all convinced there was to be an invasion. Walter left me a service revolver on the window seat in my bedroom overlooking the golf course!

Nevertheless, cricket was still being played and the one-day matches arranged at Lord's were a huge success, thanks to the efforts of Warner who declared that 'if Goebbels had been able to broadcast that the War had stopped cricket at Lord's it would have been valuable propaganda for the Germans.' Robbie appeared in four one-day matches at Lord's in August and in the match in September between a Lord's XI and a Middlesex XI.

Some children had been officially evacuated abroad to safety and other parents sought opportunities to do the same privately. Kathleen remembered: 'Walter wrote to my Uncle Arthur in California; we had met him when they were in England on holiday the year we got engaged and asked him to have the children and me and vouch for us as evacuees.' Robbie was posted to St Athan in Wales while arrangements were being made for Kathleen and the two children to travel; eventually they got to San Francisco and lived with relatives for six months in California, before continuing to Australia where they stayed with Tom Ramsay, the chairman of the Kiwi shoe polish business. He and his wife Mimi lived near Melbourne and were great friends of Kathleen and Robbie who had arranged all of Kiwi's international insurances.

Robbie was still in Wales but managed to get to Lord's for three matches in the summer of 1941 before hearing that he was being posted to Charlottetown, Prince Edward Island, on the east coast of Canada. The R.A.F. were opening a new station for training and a place for British-based pilots to be sent for 'r and r'. When Robbie arrived everything was chaotic, with practically no headquarters staff, no commanding officer and everything in process of being built, so Robbie took over. Group Captain Blake finally arrived as commanding officer to find everything under control and soon Robbie was promoted to Squadron Leader.

As soon as Walter arrived in Canada he had cabled Kathleen in Australia and suggested that she fly over to join him for a few weeks. They had not seen each other for nearly a year and she jumped at the chance, finding a boarding school for both children with arrangements for Penelope to stay with Don and Jessie Bradman during the school holidays and Charles to go back to the Ramsays. She returned to San Francisco by boat and then flew to Montreal via New York and then on to New Brunswick, where Robbie was waiting to take her to Charlottetown by R.A.F. plane. Then, on 7 December 1941, Japan attacked Pearl Harbour and Kathleen recalled:

As soon as everyone had recovered from the shock, Walter set about pulling strings to get me a passage to Australia to fetch the children back to Canada. It appeared that Australia was in peril with all their Armies and equipment overseas. Eventually I got a berth on a little Swedish freighter going out with an innocent cargo under a neutral flag. When we left New York we slipped into Newport News and took on our 'innocent cargo' which was tanks, guns and ammunition of all sorts for the US troops going to Australia. On our way down we heard by radio of the fall of Malaya and Singapore and were pretty anxious, but when we got to Sydney it was full of Yanks.

*Sqn Ldr R.W.V.Robins with colleague Douglas Smith-Bingham
in Canada in 1942.*

The dangerous voyage had taken seven weeks and Kathleen wasted no time in collecting Penelope and Charles and obtaining a passage back to San Francisco on an American troopship before going on to Canada by train. In the autumn of 1942 Robbie was posted to a new R.A.F. station at Goderich on Lake Huron and then to Picton on Lake Ontario, one of the biggest such stations in Canada, where in addition to his other duties he chaired the Victory Bond committee which raised over $55,000. As station adjutant at Picton, Robbie was determined to provide leisure time for all the young men in his charge. One of the most popular sports among the Canadians during the long winter months was, of course, ice hockey and so Robbie made arrangements to take his trainees to the local ice-rink. The eight-year-old Charles Robins was an occasional witness to his father's exploits on the ice: he 'was no skater but determined to try and master yet another sport and practised intensely, although he still found that he spent much of his time down on the ice. Refuge was at hand as he had his cricket equipment with him and strapped the thigh-pad over his backside which proved effective on many of the falls!'

The Allied campaign in North Africa had reached a triumphal conclusion and an invasion of Italy was approaching so, in the spring of 1943, Robbie was told that he would be posted back to England. He immediately put in for passages for Kathleen and the children to follow but was told that there was an indefinite wait.

Back once more in England, Robbie turned up at the nets at Lord's one Friday evening and amazed the head of the MCC groundstaff with his accurate spin-bowling, despite not having played cricket for two years. He was then able to play in a couple of games at Lord's that summer. The first was considered important enough to warrant two days at the beginning of August, and he captained an England XI against a Dominions XI, led by Keith Carmody, who had also been in Canada with the Australian air force. England scored 324 and the Dominions replied with 115. Although 209 ahead Robbie wanted to keep the game going for the entertainment of the large crowd and decided to bat again. His scheme backfired and England immediately lost four wickets for only six runs. Eventually Robbie joined Holmes at the wicket and they added 106 runs in 55 minutes. *Wisden* thought 'Robins quite in his old dashing style, made the bowling length he desired by jumping in or stepping back, and audacity brought him a six and ten fours in his 69.' The Dominions were left to make 360 to win and when 10 runs were wanted with two wickets in hand, Sismey was caught by Bedser, and off the last ball of the over Bailey caught Roper.

It wasn't until October that Kathleen could get a passage on a troopship and they sailed from Halifax in convoy to Liverpool where they were met by Robbie who took them back to London. And it was not long after that when Robbie was transferred to what he considered the best job he had during the war. The Air Ministry sent an instruction to 'all Commands' on 31 December 1943, under the heading 'A.T.C. in J.T.C. Schools, appointment of a Schools Training Officer':

A Squadron Leader post has now been established in this Directorate

Shortly after returning to England in the summer of 1943, Robbie captained this 'England' side in a two-day match against a Dominions team at Lord's. Standing (l to r): H.Gimblett, A.W.H.Mallett, T.G.Evans, L.H.Compton, A.V.Bedser, J.D.B.Robertson, T.E.Bailey. Seated: E.R.T.Holmes, R.W.V.Robins (capt), L.E.G.Ames, D.C.S.Compton.

to be filled by Squadron Leader R.W.V.Robins whose name will be familiar as that of the Middlesex and England cricketer.

Squadron Leader R.W.V.Robins will visit schools where there are contingents of both JTC and ATC. His main duty will be to discuss training problems and methods with the CO of the unit and make suggestions for improving and vitalising ATC training e.g. by making it more open air and imaginative and less of classroom kind and ensuring that all COs take advantage of facilities for visiting RAF Stations, Gliding Schools, etc which are open to them (also making sure such facilities are available). He will in general, endeavour to 'put over' the ATC training as against that of the JTC. He will in addition discuss any particular problems with the Headmaster. During school holidays he will occupy himself with NCO Courses and Training Camps.

In the meanwhile, in April 1943 the Advisory County Committee had asked MCC to appoint a Select Committee to produce a plan for post-war cricket. Robbie was asked to join that committee alongside Hammond, Wyatt, Turnbull, Sellars, Errol and Jack Holmes, Rupert Howard and Gubby Allen, under the chairmanship of Sir Stanley Jackson. Their report was published in March 1944 and 'emphasised the importance of a sound psychological approach to the game and stressed the duty of captains in particular to animate their sides into enterprise and the pursuit of a win rather than the avoidance of defeat.' Music to Robbie's ears!

In 1945, the war in Europe was reaching its end and there were plans for three two-day matches between England and the Australian Services. The first was to be at Lord's over Whitsun, then Sheffield in June and back to Lord's in August. The announcement of Victory in Europe Day on 7 May 1945 prompted MCC to upgrade the matches to first-class by adding an extra day and although it was made clear that they were not official Test matches, they soon became known as 'Victory Tests'. A third match at Lord's was slotted in for July and later the two-day Lancashire match against the Australian Services planned for Old Trafford in August was allocated a third day and renamed England versus Australian Services so that there was now a five-match series.

Robbie was asked to play in the first 'Test', at Lord's, beginning on Saturday, 19 May. According to Mark Rowe: 'It was as great a show as England cricket would ever put on. After wartime safekeeping, the paintings in the Long Room were on the walls again. Members, everyone who was anyone in cricket and public life were there.' The England team, captained by Hammond, contained seven players with Test experience: of the Australians, only the captain, Lindsay Hassett, had played Test cricket. When Robbie joined Edrich on the afternoon of the third day, England were 218 for five in their second innings, only 30 runs in front. They both began to score steadily and the game was drifting to a draw when Hammond was persuaded that the public deserved a thrilling finish. At 5.15 pm the batsmen received instructions to give away their wickets Hammond later wrote: 'I am quite confident that Robins and Edrich could have batted easily another half-hour but that would have meant a drawn game.' Both batsmen responded immediately and were out caught going for a big hit, and the last four batsmen made only seven runs between them. So, at 5.50 pm the Australians started their second innings needing to make 107 runs by stumps at 7 pm. The first two wickets fell for only 11 runs before Hassett and Pepper added 52 runs to take them nearer to the target. The 16,000 crowd kept up a continuous roar as Pepper then began to hit out at nearly every ball. At the start of the final over, the Australians needed five runs to win and just made it with two balls to spare. *The Cricketer* reported: 'A draw would have been something of an anti-climax,' and Robbie agreed that, win or lose, it was the way the game of cricket should be played. Ominously Hammond added a word of warning that the public 'cannot hope for such cricket in official Test matches. There is too much at stake.'

The year 1945 ended with the good news for the Robins family that Kathleen had given birth to another son, born on 16 November and named George Richard Vernon.

Chapter Eleven

A Fresh Start with Old Friends

Middlesex faced a problem before the first post-war season had even started when Ian Peebles decided to withdraw as captain in October 1945 but as he later reported:

> By a stroke of good luck Walter Robins was available and willing to do a couple of seasons as captain in order to get the club established again. He kindly asked me to play a few matches, partly to help out, as he was short-handed at first, and partly for old times' sake. I played about half-a-dozen games with great pleasure but to little effect, and then happily made way for younger and fitter men.

Robbie, who was 40 during the 1946 season, had also been asked to take a place on the England Selection Committee and leading Middlesex would give him the opportunity to have a first-hand look at new blood in the other counties.

Robbie's own team was certainly the strongest batting side in the country but the bowling attack looked thin, although Sims had been given early release from the Army. The County Championship had been 'rationalised' and now each county played 26 matches only, so that the positions in the table could be determined by points scored and not percentages or averages. The reduction in the number of games also provided an opportunity to introduce a knock-out competition but for the time being the idea was suspended, much to Robbie's disappointment.

When Robertson and Brown walked out to open the Middlesex innings at Lord's on the morning of the first county match, they emerged through the centre door of the pavilion. The MCC Committee had confirmed their decision to discontinue the practice of amateurs and professionals using separate dressing-rooms, thanks to the decisive action of Robbie the week before. It had been decided to have a one-day pre-season warm-up match between MCC and Middlesex and when the players assembled they automatically went to their pre-war places with the professionals changing in the Bowlers' Room and the amateurs upstairs in the No.1 Dressing Room, from where they would then meet later at the Pavilion gates when entering the field. An end to this procedure had been discussed by members of the MCC Committee the previous winter but there had been no announcement. When Robbie arrived he thought the situation was ridiculous and he immediately went downstairs to talk to the secretary, Colonel Rait Kerr, in his office. The colonel said that any decision altering such an ingrained custom had to be taken by the full MCC Committee. Robbie went back upstairs and packed his bag before returning to the Colonel's office and saying that as Squadron-Leader Bill Edrich, DFC, and

Captain Jack Robertson, amongst others who had served the country for six years, were changing downstairs, he and the amateurs were going to join them, saying 'Surely if we can fight with them we can also change with them!' Rait Kerr relented and agreed to explain to MCC what had been done in response to Robbie's intervention, so that confirmation of the new arrangements could be announced officially.

Middlesex made a great start to the season in that first game against Leicestershire: Pelham Warner reported that 'under the dynamic captaincy of Walter Robins, Middlesex were able to declare twice and force a decisive victory with 20 minutes to spare.' In the next game Northamptonshire were all out for 383 and, when Middlesex reached 384 for six, instead of building a bigger lead, Robbie immediately declared looking for a result. The visitors set Middlesex 250 runs to win and with Robbie leading the charge with an unbeaten 85, they reached 227 for nine when the umpires called time, with both sides believing they would have won if allowed to continue. By the end of May Middlesex were level in the table with Yorkshire and Lancashire but had played two games more. They lost to Yorkshire at Lord's but then won the next five consecutive games. Robbie missed the innings victory over Gloucestershire being on selector duty at Lord's for England's first Test match for seven years where they beat India by ten wickets. Four days later he was at Trent Bridge scoring his first century of the season, adding 195 for the fourth wicket with Brown and taking five for 53 in Nottinghamshire's second innings to win the match in two days. Even so, at the end of July they were trailing in third place by 20 points.

Most of the county captains had been entering into the spirit of the MCC instructions to 'animate their sides into enterprise and the pursuit of a win' but halfway through the season 'it was becoming clear that some captains were overstepping the legitimate limits of sporting cricket and conspiring to produce contrived finishes.' In July MCC announced that they had been forced to remind the county clubs of a communication issued in April 1932, stating that 'freak' declarations were not in the interests of the game or of the Championship. This may have given some captains pause for thought but Robbie was not one of them and Middlesex won six of their eight matches in August while Yorkshire and Lancashire could only win three each. He almost reached his second century for the season at The Oval against Surrey when making 93 and adding 148 for the sixth wicket with Thompson after going in at 113 for five chasing 318 and winning by four wickets. The second century came against Essex at Lord's in the last county match of 1946, but despite all this huge effort Middlesex finished runners-up to Yorkshire yet again.

Robbie played in the traditional MCC match against Yorkshire at the Scarborough festival in September where, after the first day and much of the second day had been lost to rain, he found himself going in at 63 for six and at the end of play was 21 not out at 96 for seven. On the last day he astounded everyone by launching a counter-attack on the Yorkshire bowlers and scoring 95 out of the next 96 runs and getting stumped going for another big hit at 116. It was not enough to win the match but he had the satisfaction of knowing it had been enough to prevent another Yorkshire victory. He had reached 1,000 runs for the season for the fourth time in his career, thus rather confounding Robertson-Glasgow's contention in his book *Cricket Prints* that 'with advancing years his batting technique has become more eccentric.' Jim Swanton later reported that 'Robins was still a splendid cricketer, inspiring his side with his own vitality, and always liable to make runs, take wickets or make a sensational catch, when it was most needed.'

* * * * * * *

The 1946 season was very wet with many hours of cricket, and even complete days, cancelled out by rain. This changed in 1947 when the sun shone nearly every day from May to September and, for players and supporters alike, it was time to really express their joy and relief that they had survived six years of bombs and bullets, and, according to the editor of *Wisden* 'demonstrated the great hold the game takes on spectators once they are aware that both sides and every individual mean to expend all their energies striving for a definite result.' Nearly three million spectators flocked to their favourite grounds up and down the country to watch some of the most exciting cricket ever seen. And much of it was played by Middlesex under the demanding leadership of Robbie; Denis Compton thought 'he set the tone for the all-out action the team provided.' When Middlesex were batting, 'there was excitement in the air. Men rushed from their offices to get to Lord's. Schoolboys played truant. Austerity was forgotten in clouds of happiness. It is difficult even now, 40 years on,' according to David Lemmon, writing in 1987, 'to think of those days without the pulse racing a little faster.'

Robbie couldn't play in the first four matches and his place was taken by George Mann, the son of Frank Mann, Middlesex captain from 1921 to 1928, whom he was grooming to take his place permanently the next season. After ten matches it appeared that Yorkshire were no longer in serious contention for the Championship, having won only four matches compared to Middlesex and Gloucestershire who had both won seven, leaving Middlesex top of the table with 92 points and Gloucestershire second with 88. Middlesex pushed Yorkshire even further behind by beating them on their home ground at Leeds in two days. Robbie's strategy throughout the season was working well and according to Denis Compton: 'whenever we were batting first he would announce "I want 350 plus on the board by five o'clock. Anybody unable to keep the runs coming get out and let somebody in who can."' In the last 90 minutes of the first day's play, he expected his bowlers to make a significant breakthrough and set up a victory.

By 13 August Middlesex had a chance to take the lead in the title race when they met Kent at Lord's. When the visitors declared their second innings closed they left Middlesex a mere four hours and twenty minutes to score 397 runs for the win they needed. This meant scoring at nearly 92 runs an hour with most of the Kent fieldsmen posted on the boundary. Both Robertson and Brown went quickly and there was little hope of reaching the target. Most teams would have settled for a draw at that stage in preference to going for the runs and risking defeat, but before Denis Compton went in to bat, he thought he should hear his captain's view on the situation and asked what he should do. Robbie's reply was typically direct: 'Go for the bloody runs, of course!' Needing no further encouragement, Compton and Mann proceeded to hit 161 runs in 98 minutes but eventually, still going for the runs, Compton's wicket fell to Wright for a magnificent 168 and Middlesex lost by 75 runs.

The most vital game of the season came next at Cheltenham. Gloucestershire now held a four point lead and both sides had played 21 games. The odds favoured the home side as Middlesex would be without Compton and Robertson, who were both playing in the Fifth Test, and Edrich was unable to bowl due to a shoulder injury. Excitement was in the air: 'The ground was filled to capacity an hour before the start. The weather was magnificent, the setting beautiful and the atmosphere electric.' Wickets fell rapidly on the first day and Middlesex obtained a first innings lead of 27. Before starting their second innings ten minutes before the close of play, Robbie told his openers Brown and Edrich to see out play but Edrich was soon out lbw to Goddard and so he sent in Sharp as nightwatchman. On the Monday morning the Cheltenham College ground was again bursting at the seams. Brown was bowled early by Goddard, and Robins, 'always the first up the ladder when a castle was to be stormed', joined Sharp. They added 70 runs but the innings ended leaving Gloucestershire needing 168 runs to win. The home side made steady progress to 67 for three before Robbie decided it was time to switch from leg-spin to off-breaks and he tossed the ball to Sharp with the instruction, 'Just keep it tight.' Sharp did more than that and took three wickets for the addition of only seven runs before Gloucestershire crashed all out for 100, well short of victory. Before the fall of the last wicket, Robbie called the team together and said that at the conclusion he wanted no victory celebrations, but they should walk off the field as if they never doubted any other result.

Two more wins followed and when Northamptonshire came to Lord's on 27 August Middlesex were just twelve points away from the title. At 7.05 pm on Thursday, 28 August, Middlesex became the champion county after an inspirational declaration by Mann in typical Robbie style. Robbie may not have been there for the fulfilment of his dream but everyone knew who was the architect of the great achievement. In Roy Webber's words, 'has always led the way for "brighter" (or I prefer, more positive) cricket and this summer was a vindication of his methods. Few post-war captains have been so quick to get a stranglehold on a match as Robins was that season.' Denis Compton put it: 'We were a good side and Robins never forgot to remind us of that fact. But he also hammered into us that there could be no let-up. He demanded all-out effort from everybody all day and every day.'

Some historians have since disparaged the success of Middlesex in 1947 as having been achieved on the backs of the incredible batting of Compton and Edrich. But John Arlott has pointed out that 'of the nine matches they played at less than full strength — on occasions Young and Robertson were taken for Test matches as well as Compton and Edrich — they won seven.' Of the five occasions when Middlesex were beaten, 'three were through continuing to attack a large fourth innings objective, rather than accept a "safe" draw.' In mid July, against Somerset at Taunton, when left 369 runs to win on the last day, Robbie was asked, 'You're not going for the runs are you?' and he replied, 'Not 'arf ... !' and their tenth wicket fell 25 runs short of the target with ten minutes still left for play. With or without his star players, Robbie always expected to win. According to Christopher Martin-Jenkins, an old Middlesex player was once asked, 'What difference did Walter Robins make to a match?' He replied, 'The difference between the quick and the dead.'

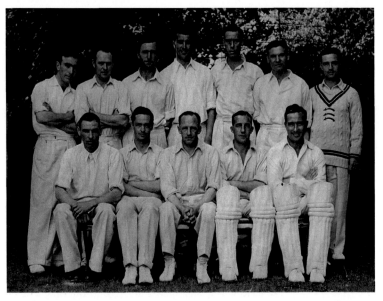

The well-known photograph of the Middlesex side which won the County Championship in 1947. Standing (l to r): J.T.Eaglestone, A.W.Thompson, J.D.B.Robertson, L.H.Compton (wk), L.H.Gray, S.M.Brown, J.A.Young. Seated: J.M.Sims, F.G.Mann, R.W.V.Robins (capt), W.J.Edrich, D.C.S.Compton. Robbie led the side in 18 of its 26 matches.

But there was still one more match for Middlesex to play that season, the four-day Champion County versus The Rest of England at The Oval. England's Test captain, Norman Yardley, led The Rest which was filled with players from the summer's successful Test series against South Africa and expected to give Robbie and his merry men a real test. Winning the toss, Robbie was able to declare on the second day at 543 for nine, thanks to 246 from Compton and 189 from Edrich, and after making The Rest follow on, won by nine wickets. The champion county had won this fixture only twice before.

* * * * * * *

Still a Test selector, but with business commitments that would not allow him to play as regularly as he would have wished, Robbie handed over the Middlesex captaincy to George Mann in December 1947. But it wasn't just the need to spend more time in the office that would keep him off the field of play, he was going to be the overseer of the arrangements for the Australian touring team from April to September, including a series of five Test matches. He would reserve the hotel accommodation and organise the travelling between matches, as well as the itinerary for all official social engagements. The Australians were being led by Don Bradman and so the two friends were going to be able to spend plenty of time together. In fact, if it had not been for their friendship it is unlikely that Bradman would have decided to take on such a responsibility which he confirmed in a letter to Robbie in February 1948:

> Before the end of this week I am going to announce publicly that I am available to go to England as a player in 1948. That means you are absolutely right (for the first time I can remember) that there is sentiment in cricket, for nothing but sentiment is taking me back to England. Your letter played a big part in my decision. You are the best pal I have made in the cricket world, and without you on the other side I doubt whether I could have faced it. I am anxious that this tour will be the greatest success of all time. We'll do our best to beat you fair and square but we don't want any hard feelings or post mortems. I feel that you can do an enormous amount towards helping.

Soon after Bradman arrived in April, ten days before the opening match at Worcester, he spent a weekend at Burnham Beeches with the Robins family, but alone this time as Jessie had remained at home in Adelaide. This was still 'austerity Britain' where many people were grateful to receive food parcels to augment their rations from relatives and friends overseas. Don had brought with him two large wooden crates full of food and goodies from Australia. Charles Robins says he picked 'them out individually and distributed them, like Father Christmas. My mother insisted we indulge him with thanks and praise, which he loved!' For Bradman there was a seat at Wembley for the FA Cup Final between Manchester United and Blackpool, an invitation to the service at St Paul's Cathedral to commemorate the silver wedding anniversary of King George VI and Queen Elizabeth, plus opportunities to speak at the Sportsman's Club, Institute of Journalists and the Cricket Writers' Club. Bradman was a great anglophile who was putting his reputation and health at risk by coming on this tour, but he could think of no more appropriate place to end his Test career.

Jack Holmes continued as chairman of the England Test selectors, with Johnnie Clay, captain of Glamorgan, and Robbie, as before, but because of the importance of the Ashes series, another member was added, Brian Sellers of Yorkshire, so that there would be more up-to-date personal assessments of players form and performance. Despite the success of England during the series against South Africa the previous summer under the capable captaincy of Norman Yardley, there was a growing feeling in some quarters that a more adventurous leadership was needed if England were going to recover the Ashes. If anyone was capable of putting pressure on Bradman then it had to be Robbie, so the argument went, and his brilliant management the previous season of the Middlesex team including Compton and Edrich was all the proof that was needed. Robbie himself would not be drawn into the debate but kept his options open by playing in four of the first six county matches at Lord's under the leadership of Mann.

In the meantime, the Australian had been travelling around the counties demonstrating the quality of their batting, bowling and fielding, and making it very clear what a huge task England would face when the Test matches started. They had won seven of their first ten matches by an innings and Bradman himself had already scored 759 runs at an average of 94.37, including three centuries. But first it was time for a Test Trial at Edgbaston where Yardley would lead an England XI and Ken Cranston, the Lancashire skipper, would be captain of The Rest. Robbie decided to take his selection duties seriously and took a place in the Rest eleven under Cranston, in order to check at close quarters the form of those in the running for places in the England team. Rain reduced the game to less than an innings each and little was learned, so the selectors decided that Yardley should stay in place and Robbie went off to play for Middlesex at Lord's against Yorkshire. After that, for the next seven weeks he concentrated exclusively on the first four Ashes Tests.

Australia won the First Test at Nottingham by eight wickets and the Second, at Lord's, by 409 runs, as the selectors looked on and wondered what they could do to stem the tide. Meanwhile, Bradman rushed his team to complete a victory over Surrey during the morning of the last day of the match, so that they could take up an invitation to watch the Men's Singles final at Wimbledon in the afternoon. He then sent them off to Bristol to play Gloucestershire while he relaxed with the Robins family for a few days, dining and chatting, and playing some golf with Robbie.

It was no secret that England were going to make changes for the Third Test at Old Trafford. The selectors were particularly concerned about how Bradman had concentrated the bounce and pace of Lindwall, Miller and Johnston against Hutton and that at Lord's Hutton had, in *Wisden*'s later words, 'looked plainly uncomfortable'. There were murmurs of discontent from within the ranks of MCC members seeing what appeared to be an alarming loss of confidence, and it was a situation that the selectors could not ignore. The decision was made and Hutton's omission from the Third Test eleven sent shock-waves around the country, despite being only one of four changes deemed necessary. The new line-up worked and at the end of the third day England were 316 runs in front with seven wickets in hand. The whole of the fourth day was washed out and on the morning of the final day Yardley declared immediately to give his bowlers an opportunity to dismiss the Australians who would be without the injured Barnes. After half an hour Australia lost Johnson, the stand-in opener, but showers curtailed play and Morris and Bradman stuck it out.

The opportunity for England to win back the Ashes was gone but at least it looked as if it was possible to win the last two Tests and share the series. The last thing anyone expected was that the selectors would throw the opportunity away by forgetting that the wicket at Leeds was certain to favour spin, preferably sharp and from the leg, and England had several bowlers, all fit and available to take advantage of such conditions. Instead they picked the off-spinner Laker. At least they brought back Hutton, who had scored two centuries and averaged 88.20 from six innings between the Second and Fourth Tests. He now shared two century opening partnerships with Washbrook to help put England into a commanding position on the final day when Yardley, hoping for an Australian collapse, declared after just two more overs and asked them to try and make 404 runs to win in just five and a half hours play, a feat never before accomplished on the fifth day of Anglo-Australian Tests. The runs came slowly at first but, after Hassett was out for 17, Morris and Bradman added 301 runs in 217 minutes before Morris was out, soon followed by Miller. Bradman went on to an undefeated 173 runs when Harvey hit the winning boundary with 14 minutes to spare: Robbie was ashamed to admit that he and other selectors 'waited until it was dark and slipped out of a side gate.'

Now the idea of a recall for Robbie as England captain was the hot topic of conversation among England supporters once again. As Alan Gibson noted, 'it was felt that Robins, still a fine player, might have brought a touch of dash and adventure which would have enabled England to end the season on a brighter note.' Whether the other selectors took this seriously or not, Robbie returned immediately to the ranks of Middlesex and played in the next four championship matches. But the selectors remained faithful to Yardley for the final Test and Robbie stayed away from another crushing defeat at The Oval, to go off and play against Kent at Dover, hitting 101 in the first innings and 74 out of 203 in the second to help Middlesex win by six wickets.

There were two more championship matches to play before what would be for Robbie the biggest event of the season. He would captain the Gentlemen of England XI against the Australian tourists in Bradman's last match at Lord's, which would also be Bradman's fortieth birthday. It must have been an emotional moment for them both as they walked out to the middle to toss for innings. Bradman chose correctly and elected to bat on a perfect wicket, going in to treat the spectators to a magnificent innings of 150 and then sacrificing his wicket by lofting a ball from Brown to Donnelly in the deep. Before walking through the doors of the Long Room for the last time as a batsman, he took off his gloves, hung them around his bat handle, raised them high, removed his cap and bowed farewell, first to the crowd, then to the members in the pavilion.

Before Bradman returned to Australia there was one last official function. A luncheon was arranged at the Savoy Hotel in his honour, attended by a host of dignitaries and players who had competed against him. He was presented with a replica of the 2,000-year-old Warwick Vase found in Rome by Sir William Hamilton, the cost of the gift having been raised by an appeal in *The People* newspaper. There was a considerable amount left over and the paper wanted to give him a cheque, but Robbie was delighted when he learned that his friend had asked that the money should be used to lay concrete pitches in parks in England for the benefit of young cricketers. There was reason for even more celebration in the Robins family when Kathleen had their fourth child in November, named Unity, after the wife of Nigel Haig.

Robbie in action in the immediate post-war seasons.

Chapter Twelve
The Spirit of Middlesex Undimmed

Robbie continued as an England selector in 1949 but was disappointed that the New Zealand tourists had only been allocated three days for each of their four Test matches. He attended the First Test at Leeds but quickly realised that the sides were evenly matched and unlikely to break the deadlock within the time allowed. He thought the situation was ridiculous and decided that he would be more valuable to Mann and Middlesex in another attempt to win the Championship. He was unable to start playing until June but managed to fit in twelve county matches between his Test match duties as selector. The last county match of the season was against Derbyshire at Lord's. Victory would put Middlesex at the top of the table and make them champions if Yorkshire lost their last match a few days later. The visitors bowled Middlesex out for 139, Robbie top-scoring with 45, to take a lead of 89 and went on to set Middlesex 193 to win. It was Robbie to the rescue again, joining Compton at 36 for five. They added 90 runs in 70 minutes, 50 of them from Robbie, and went on to win by three wickets with Compton 97 not out. But Yorkshire won at Newport and so the two counties shared the title.

Robbie's last appearance that summer was in a one-day match at Bournemouth in aid of the National Playing Fields Association. He was playing against Hampshire for the Duke of Edinburgh's Eleven which also included Gubby Allen, Freddie Brown, Denis Compton, Errol Holmes, Billy Griffith, Tom Goddard and the Duke himself, president of the NPFA, who won by one wicket, thanks in part to Robbie's unbeaten 35. The Robins family stayed on in Dorset for a few days and Robbie, Vivian and Charles were invited to play golf at Studland Bay Golf Club. Charles recalls the unexpected end to their visit:

> Having completed our morning round, I threw a golf ball for a catch wide of my grandfather which ricocheted against the picket fence surrounding the small clubhouse where a few were enjoying pre-lunch drinks on deckchairs, tables etc. One elderly matron rose and came over to the fence and asked me, aged 14, what I was doing. I explained my error and apologised which I think she had accepted, when RWV appeared fuming after missing his putt, and then practice putt, on the eighteenth green: 'The boy's apologized ... what more do you want?' With that she opened the gate and there followed the most amazing couple of minutes of pure fury. RWV never swore and was pretty good 'off the cuff' but he'd met his match! The next day when we turned up to play, the Secretary, a retired Wing Commander who knew RWV from the RAF, was very apologetic but said that the owner had banned him from the course and there was nothing he could do, but as she was

leaving the following day, he would be welcome any day that she was not around. That lady was Enid Blyton!

The famous author of children's books had indeed bought the club that year, with her husband Dr Kenneth Darrell-Waters, and might have been a little more understanding if she had known that, earlier that year, the MCC Youth Cricket Association had been formed under the chairmanship of Harry Altham, with Robbie on the committee. The purpose was to examine problems concerning the learning and playing of cricket by young people in Britain from 11 to 17 and to consider how best to foster their enthusiasm. The Association started the coaching school at Lilleshall where every autumn an advanced coaching course was offered, ending with the Advanced Coaching Certificate being awarded to successful candidates.

During that summer of 1949, Mann had indicated that it would be his last regular season and that Middlesex needed to find a replacement captain. No full-time volunteer came forward and Mann agreed to continue in 1950. Later, though, he withdrew his acceptance and Robbie stepped into the breach, but could play in only ten of the 28 championship fixtures, with the leadership in other games shared out between four players.

Robbie's attention during June was focussed more on the progress of his eldest son, Charles, playing his first season for Eton College and taking wickets in much the same numbers as his father had done at Highgate. To check things out first-hand he put together a team for the Forty Club and went down to Eton to play the College first eleven. The Forty Club had been formed in 1936 with the aim 'to take cricket to the schools' by offering schools, both state and public, fixtures against experienced cricketers who would encourage the young cricketers to play the game to the highest standards of performance and behaviour. Robbie proceeded to knock all the young Eton bowlers about, including Charles, before being run out for 71, and when it was Eton's turn to bat, he took the catch that dismissed Charles who had scored 27, going in at eighth wicket down and leading a fight-back while still more than a hundred runs short of victory. Learning from this experience, Charles continued to take more wickets for the College and was chosen to play in the traditional fixture against Harrow, so that Robbie dropped out of the Middlesex games at Worcester and Leeds to be at Lord's to give his support and encouragement.

Robbie was back leading Middlesex in August, steering them to away wins at Leicester and Hove. His last game that summer was at Lord's when his top score of 58 out of 161 in the second innings against Surrey could not prevent a loss by six wickets. Without the continuity of a regular captain Middlesex slumped to fourteenth in the table, winning only five of their 28 matches. Ian Peebles commented: 'At least the spirit of Middlesex under Walter Robins was undimmed, and even in the prevailing adversity he maintained a lively, positive attitude whatever the state of the game.' After the season had ended business took Robbie to New York and Australia, where he saw some of the Ashes series. He even bowled in the nets to help batsmen struggling with Iverson's 'mysteries'.

* * * * * * *

In 1951 the Canadian Cricket Association invited MCC to send an amateur team to Canada to encourage further development and popularity of the game.

The tour was not scheduled to start until the beginning of August but, even so, Robbie played only two first-class matches in England before leaving. He played once for Middlesex under the captaincy of Bill Edrich at Lord's against Hampshire in May, and in June went with the Free Foresters to Cambridge to play the University. Fenner's was a noted featherbed in those days and Robbie said he could make a hundred on it with a walking stick. Gubby Allen went in to hit an entertaining 103 but when it was his turn, Robbie was bowled first ball by John Warr in the first innings and again in the second, to suffer the fourth 'king-pair' of his career. Teddy Unwin, who followed him in both innings, and on a hat-trick both times, said as they passed the second time: 'I'm getting rather bored with this!'

Two weeks later, accompanied by his brother Vernon, Robbie went to Eton College to play for the Forty Club again. On this occasion this time the dismissal of young Charles was kept within the family and he was caught by his uncle off Robbie's bowling. But there was still time for a proud father to watch his son play at Lord's in his second Eton and Harrow match, when he was delighted to see him take thirteen wickets, eight for 29 in the first innings and five for 62 in the second, when Harrow managed to reach 167 for nine and escape with a draw, still 105 runs behind.

On 24 July, the touring party of fourteen sailed from Liverpool to Canada. Robbie had been appointed captain and he was pleased that the party included young John Warr who had already had played with him for Middlesex. Warr never forgot the experience of playing under Robbie: 'He would subject the batsman to a non-stop running commentary on the current state of the game, the percentage of luck he considered he was getting and the inadequacies of his own bowling.' The team was scheduled to play 22 matches in six weeks and would visit twelve towns and cities. Robbie knew that Canadians had been brought up on a diet of baseball and that to sell them the game of cricket it would be vital that MCC fielding was as athletic as possible, so he ordered extra practice sessions before every game.

In Toronto they played a three-day first-class match against Canada which MCC won by 141 runs and then travelled to Montreal for the last two games, in the second of which, against a Montreal West Indian eleven, Robbie hit his second century of the tour. The visit has largely been reported as successful: R.S.Rait Kerr thought the team 'brought enormous pleasure and encouragement' and 'delighted their hosts with their aggressive play'. More recently though, it has been said that there was dissent in the party over Robbie's approach to discipline and his insistence on slaughtering club-standard opposition.

Chapter Thirteen
Changing the Law

At the Advisory County Cricket Committee meeting at Lord's in March 1952 it was proposed that a sub-committee be appointed to examine the state of county cricket. Counties had become concerned about falling attendances, and the fact that in 1951 more than 50% of county matches had finished as draws, and there was a growing public demand for more attractive cricket. MCC gave wholehearted support to the Advisory's proposal and the MCC Cricket sub-committee, of which Robbie was a member, began by giving serious consideration to possible amendments to the leg-before-wicket Law, in particular to proposals from Don Bradman over the previous nineteen years. His first suggestion had been made in a two-page typewritten letter to the MCC secretary, dated 30 January 1933. This would have arrived at Lord's soon after the Bodyline crisis had been temporarily resolved to allow the 1932/33 Ashes series to be completed. In the meantime MCC had advised the Australian Board of Control that the Committee 'will watch carefully during the present season for anything which might be regarded as unfair or prejudicial to the best interest of the game. They propose to invite opinions and suggestions from county clubs and captains at the end of the season with a view to enabling them to express an opinion on this matter at a special meeting of the Imperial Cricket Conference.' A private letter 'out-of-the-blue' from the batsman who had been one of the main targets for England's leg-theory tactics during the recent Test series, asking MCC to take a fresh look at the lbw Law and not the problems of Bodyline, appears to have been treated as being a subject that had no relevance to the investigations proposed, and so it was ignored and placed on file without even the courtesy of an acknowledgement.

But by 1934 MCC was prepared to re-examine the lbw Law, although without any reference to Bradman's earlier suggestion, and produced an experimental amendment to be used for a trial period during the 1935 season. It didn't go quite as far as Bradman would have liked, but was a step in the right direction as it extended the Law to allow an umpire to give a batsman out after missing a ball pitching on the off-side of the wicket provided it hit some part of the striker between wicket and wicket. Wilfrid Brookes, the editor of the 1936 *Wisden*, asked several people to give their opinion and Robbie wrote:

> I am a firm believer that, if the experiment becomes law, we shall go a long way towards obtaining 'brighter' cricket. Our wicket at Lord's last year gave the rule as big a test as any other ground in the country and in no case did I hear an umpire during the whole season suggest that it made his duties more difficult. On the contrary, many agreed that it

lightened their task. It is up to the rest of the cricketing counties and all Club Cricket Associations to try the experiment thoroughly without delay. We in Middlesex were delighted with the experiment and think that it has given a very much needed fillip to the game.

The trial was continued for another season and in 1937 Law 24 was amended.

For the 1939 *Wisden* Brookes invited Bradman to contribute an article on the future of the game and he used the opportunity to stress that he believed that it was time for another change to the law:

> Irrespective of where the batsman's pads or feet are, I believe that if a ball is pitched in a line between wicket and wicket, or on the off-side of the wicket and would have hit the stumps but is prevented from doing so by part of the batsman's person (providing the ball has not first touched his bat or hand) the bowler is entitled to be rewarded. Under the existing law, that part of the batsman's person which is struck by the ball *must be between wicket and wicket.*

Bradman thought those last six words afford the batsman too much latitude. He went on to say that the 'leg-side may have to be considered in later years, but it would probably be too drastic a step to alter both sides at once.'

During the correspondence between Robbie and Bradman over the years, the subject of the lbw law had frequently been mentioned and in 1951 Bradman had been able to find a copy of his 1933 letter to MCC. Signing off as 'Goldie' he wrote to Robbie as follows:

> I promised you that I would try and find the letter I wrote to MCC. I did so and a copy is enclosed. It was written in Jan 1933 in the middle of the test match season. No reply was received. You may remember that Larwood said at one time 'inter alia' that he had to resort to leg side bowling because he was wasting his time bowling at or outside the off stump. Batsmen were so adept at covering up with their pads that he could beat a man but not get his wicket. This statement impressed me not so much a reason as an excuse for body-line and was one of the reasons why I then said to myself — alright — take away this excuse and then where would be his argument for the leg side. Apparently I was not alone in my thoughts for if you turn to page 309 of the 1933 Wisden you will find the editor has therein written 'To the abuse of this law (i.e. lbw) may fairly be traced the trouble which has arisen in Australia during our tour now in progress'. He then went on to advocate a return to the original lbw law 'with qualifications as to its application on the leg side'.

You will notice in one part of my letter that I refer to the 'snick' in the lbw law. That, of course, has since been abolished and rightly so. Now you rocked me a bit the other day when you asked why I had not done anything to try and bring about this alteration. I replied by telling you that the MCC made the laws of cricket and that unless they were prepared to try the experiment then it just had no hope of succeeding. That is correct. I wrote to MCC in 1933. Apparently my letter and my views were consigned to the dustbin. Anyway in those days who, amongst the greybeards of England or Aust. thought I was qualified to talk about the laws of the game. In 1939 I wrote an article in Wisden and I commend to you the views I therein expressed — page 44 — in fact the whole article. In Australia I persuaded the S.A. Cricket Assoc'n to experiment with the lbw law and we played district cricket under it one or two seasons. The experiment in my opinion was a success but it was abandoned because (a) it was felt that our players were at a big disadvantage playing under one rule in club cricket and another one in inter-state cricket and (b) the other states refused even to try the experiment. No doubt, the batsmen, who are in the majority, opposed it. If you will read the 1936 Wisden, page 341, you will find a most illuminating argument about the lbw. It shows clearly how the present off-side extension was opposed by many including Sutcliffe but that the fears were swept away by 'genuine methods in the art of batsmanship.

You will need to work carefully because the majority of batsmen will oppose a change for selfish reasons. But we must remember the public view and above all the game itself. Surely the experiment could be tried in the same way as the last one was tried — see how many decisions it brings — signal lbw (n) — if both countries try it simultaneously. If MCC will try I'll bet I can get our people to do likewise but without MCC we won't do anything. So good luck.

So in 1952 Robbie was able to refer back to Bradman's earlier correspondence and begin a campaign to persuade the MCC Cricket Sub-committee to implement Bradman's proposal. But Robbie was also concerned about slow play and time-wasting which was even beginning to affect cricket played at schools and he sent a list of radical suggestions to the MCC secretary, Ronny Aird:

1 Too much first-class cricket.
2 Suggest two divisions on association football lines with a limit of twenty matches per county per season.
3 Lack of playing facilities for elementary [sic] and secondary schoolboys.
   Suggest provision of concrete pitches in parks. (Of course a great deal has been done on this direction.)
4 Standard of Coaching. Safety-first tactics used by first-class cricket coaches, and most schoolmasters.
5 Suggest we are too technical, defence is the main consideration instead of attack.
6 Boys are in danger of being coached on mass production lines rather than personality and individuality being considered.
7 Lack of amateurs of the right quality.
8 Suggest although cricket technique may have improved over the past fifty years, the 'spirit' has declined. Public schoolboys be encouraged to turn professional at attractive wages in some form.'

Coinciding with the MCC issuing a book and a film on coaching, to which he had contributed, Robbie took his own steps, rarely recalled these days, to find schoolboy cricketers with the right aptitudes. He persuaded Billy Butlin to award a 'Young Cricketer of the Week' at his holiday camps throughout the summer. Those selected were rewarded with a free week's coaching at Filey, the finale being a two-day match against a Public Schools XI. Charles Robins captained the latter side in 1952, but recalled that as soon as we looked like winning [Robbie] insisted that we hold back as the whole scheme would thus be put in jeopardy!'

Robbie (left) with Billy Butlin and Lady Isobel Barnett.
Butlin's holiday camps ran cricket coaching as part of Robbie's effort
to extend public interest in the game.

Robbie was also asked in 1952 to take over as captain of the Middlesex Second Eleven, then playing in the Minor Counties Championship. The desperate need for new young players had now been recognised and attempts were being made to develop youth cricket in the county. Robbie was approached by J.W.Hearne who asked whether he could be of any use in connection with the coaching of the young players. Robbie was very enthusiastic about the idea and gave warm support to the plan to employ Hearne to supervise coaching in Middlesex practice nets on Tuesday and Thursday evenings, as well as attending Second Eleven matches with a view to relating mistakes made in matches to net practice. The Seconds matches were all of two days' duration and the perfect platform for Robbie to demonstrate to his young protégés the need for fast scoring and sharp minds to search out victories from creative declarations.

He interrupted his appearances with the Second Eleven in June by taking another Forty Club team down to Eton College. This time young Charles found himself facing not only his father and uncle, but his 71-year-old grandfather, Vivian, as well! Charles was caught behind the wicket off the bowling of his uncle but ensured victory for the College by taking two late wickets, including that of his grandfather. Three weeks later the Robins family gathered at Lord's to see the Eton versus Harrow match, but the atmosphere was a little quieter than usual. 'The young supporters of Eton College were unable to attend the match as a fatal case of poliomyelitis had brought medical precautions into play. Over the two days the teams lunched and took tea in separate rooms.' But there was nothing muted about the enthusiasm of the Harrow supporters when their team, according to R.S.Rait Kerr:

> undaunted by a brilliant spell of bowling by Charles Robins, swept to victory by seven wickets at 2.30 pm on the second day. The early finish enabled a large crowd to throng the Long Room and see the recently discovered Eton Upper Club score-book of 1805, containing the score of the first match between the schools, with Lord Byron playing for Harrow, who on that occasion, in the poet's words, were most confoundedly beat.

* * * * * * *

The Australian were due to tour England in 1953 and once again Robbie was asked to organise all the travel arrangements and hotel reservations before they arrived in April. Everything was agreed more easily than five years before, although there were initial complications when the liner *S.S.Orcades* bringing the tourists was held up by engine trouble and landed at Tilbury ten days late. After that hiccup Robbie was able to turn his attention to something much closer to home.

The legendary Staffordshire and England cricketer, Sydney Barnes, reached his eightieth birthday that year and Stafford Cricket Club decided that it was a milestone to be celebrated. Barnes still worked as an engrosser of important documents and lived in Penkridge, about five miles south of Stafford. As well as travelling down to London every year to attend the Lord's Test as an honorary MCC member he was collected from his home by volunteer chauffeurs and taken to matches at The Hough, Stafford's home ground. He would sit in the same place every week, hardly ever speaking to anyone, but watching the cricket intently, never taking his eye off the action all day. His birthday was due on 19 April, so the club organised a testimonial one-day match a week later between an S.F.Barnes XI, captained by Robbie, and an England XI captained by Norman Yardley.

Over 500 runs were scored on the day and the 5,000 spectators who packed the ground were entertained by half-centuries from Denis Compton, Jack Robertson, Reg Simpson, Norman Yardley and Charles Palmer, but the biggest cheer was reserved for Barnes himself after opening the bowling with a maiden over before retiring to his favourite seat in the pavilion. The Stafford Cricket Club commissioned a portrait of Barnes which was presented to MCC the following year and continues to hang in the pavilion at Lord's.

Soon after the match at Stafford, Robbie and his brother took a Forty Club side to Eton again, where Charles now faced them as captain; he went on to lead the school to victory over Harrow at Lord's after scoring a century in Eton's first innings. The only other appearances by Robbie that year were

*Charles Robins on his way to 102 for Eton against Harrow at Lord's in 1953.
In first-class cricket he had success as a bowler.*

*The Shrubbery House at Froyle in Hampshire,
the Robins family home from 1953 to 1963.*

four matches leading the Middlesex seconds. This should have allowed Robbie plenty of time to follow England's fortunes which culminated in winning back the Ashes in Coronation Year under the professional captain, Len Hutton, but he was often otherwise engaged. He and Kathleen had found an ideal property at Froyle in north-east Hampshire, a small village astride the old Pilgrim's Way from Winchester to Canterbury and about 50 miles from London. 'The Shrubbery' was a large house, partly eighteenth-century, with a walled garden and meadows rolling down to the banks of the River Wey, but it was in a bad state of repair. So in 1953 they moved into the adjoining cottage until all the renovation work had been completed. There was also plenty of work to be done in the garden and grounds, but until a gardener was engaged Kathleen recalled that 'Walter threw his heart and soul into the garden, cutting down trees, sawing wood, working the machines on lawns and meadow, and gravelling the paths and patios.' Later that year the house was ready for them but not long after they had moved in, Robbie's father Vivian had a heart attack and had to leave his flat at Belsize Park, where he had lived since Mabel passed away in 1950. He took up permanent residence in the cottage, from where he was soon back on his feet and going to the office in London two or three times a week.

* * * * * * *

By the start of the 1954 season Robbie was back as a member of the England Selection Committee, working to put together a team to win a four-Test series against Pakistan, then new kids on the block, but also looking for the right team, and captain, to send to Australia the following winter capable of retaining the Ashes.

Hutton's success as captain in the previous summer had been tarnished by events in the West Indies during the MCC tour that followed, when he was criticised for the use of defensive bowling wide of leg stump in the First Test. Eventually Hutton confounded his critics by winning two of the last three Tests to square the series, but back in England there were those who continued to regard Hutton's overall leadership as far too defensive and unsuitable to lead an MCC tour to Australia. His detractors wanted the captaincy to go to David Sheppard who, in the previous summer, had spurred Sussex into second place in the Championship with youthful zest and had demonstrated undoubted flair for leadership.

For reasons that he doesn't explain, Alan Gibson wrote later that it was Robbie acting alone 'who tried, in 1954, to replace Hutton by Sheppard as the England captain, and did it in a cloak-and-dagger way', suggesting that he was working independently from the other selectors. Although it isn't hard to imagine that Robbie would have been outspoken in his criticisms of any negative tactics employed by Hutton, 'cloak-and-dagger' was never his style, and in any case, some of the other selectors may have been nursing their own doubts about the suitability of Hutton. Within MCC, Warner was certainly one of a group who favoured Sheppard, and he encouraged C.B.Fry to write an article in *The Cricketer* in which it was assumed that recent developments had made Sheppard's place certain. In fact, it was Ronny Aird, the MCC secretary, not Robbie, who secretly approached Sheppard to discuss the captaincy of England as Sheppard revealed in *Parson's Pitch*: 'We went to conspiratorial lengths to prevent anyone knowing that we were discussing anything. I was to go to his home rather than to his office and he would leave the door open so that I could walk straight in.' As a result of those clandestine meetings Sheppard agreed to suspend his theological training to make himself available if he was wanted as captain on the Australian tour. This arrangement was soon uncovered and the press had a field day publishing arguments for and against Hutton as captain.

Fuel was added to the flames of conjecture when the selectors announced that they had appointed Hutton as captain only for the First Test against Pakistan. Heavy and continuous rain prevented any play on the first three days at Lord's and until 3.45 pm of the afternoon of the fourth day. Despite nearly six hours play on the final day nothing had been resolved, so the selectors re-appointed Hutton for a further single Test. However, Hutton was now advised by his doctors to take a prolonged holiday from cricket and Sheppard was asked to step in and captain England for the next two Tests, at Nottingham and Manchester. Many assumed that this must mean that a decision had been made to replace Hutton as captain for the tour of Australia but Sheppard still had doubts: 'It was an unpleasant position to be in, because I felt quite unsure of my position, as though I was more of a caretaker than a captain. Almost as soon as I was appointed captain I sensed the tide of feelings was running the other way.' His suspicions were confirmed by Robbie who had the courage to tell him personally that the situation had changed: 'Walter Robins, who was a selector, came to my hotel room in Nottingham during the Test match and said "I feel we've been unfair to Len. He was in a very difficult position in the West Indies."' When the team for Australia was chosen during the weekend of the Manchester Test, with Gubby Allen and Charles Palmer joining the selection committee, Sheppard already knew he wasn't going to go. Hutton was re-appointed captain, starting with the last Test against Pakistan at The Oval, and Sheppard returned to his theological training at Ridley Hall.

For Robbie at least the trials of selecting were lessened in mid June, between the First and Second Tests, when he played alongside his son Charles for MCC against Cambridge University at Lord's. Between them they took nine of the 14 Cambridge wickets which fell; with *Wisden* offering the opinion that they 'bowled astutely for the losers'.

* * * * * * *

Despite the doubts over Hutton's leadership, England retained the Ashes in the winter of 1954/55. Robbie withdrew from the selection committee feeling that his job was done, but he continued to exchange letters with Bradman concerning their ideas for changes to the lbw law. They discussed the matter at length during Don's visits to England in 1956 to cover the Ashes series for the *Daily Mail*, when once again Robbie had organised all the transport and hotel bookings for the Australians. That autumn the Altham Committee began a series of meetings to consider options covering every factor in the conduct of the game which might serve to enliven its tempo. The discussions also ranged over possible reforms in the structure of first-class cricket and possible changes to the lbw law. Finally the Altham Committee presented its report in January 1957 rejecting the 'Bradman' extension giving a batsman out if he padded up and made no attempt to play a ball which would have hit the wicket, even if the point of impact were outside the line of wicket and wicket, because of the difficulties it would present to umpires in interpreting the batsman's intentions.

There was no progress on any of the other proposed changes to the status quo of cricket during 1957 and when the summer of 1958 arrived Robbie's priorities were of a much more personal nature — the wedding reception at The Shrubbery for his daughter Penelope and Major Ken Came of the Parachute Regiment.

Later that year Robbie played his 379th and last first-class match. It began on 6 September in Dublin when he led an MCC touring eleven against Ireland in a three-day match at College Park. Colin Cowdrey found the opportunity of playing in a match with him an unforgettable experience:

> Robins was captain. Now in his fifties he fielded at mid off, bowled a few erratic but highly entertaining overs of leg-breaks, batted number eleven, wore his MCC cap and never stopped talking about himself and the cricket and cricketers of his era. He was the unforgettable character of an entertaining week-end: witty, dominant, charming, magnetic. By the time we had returned to London I had fallen under his spell.

That winter Peter May was the captain of the England team that went to Australia to defend the Ashes and lost 4-0. It was in this series that the problems of bowlers 'throwing' was first highlighted. No official complaints were made but the English press complained loudly about the 'chuckers'. Robbie was more concerned about the negative tactics being employed by the England team and after the Third Test wrote to Don:

> Australia two up and two to go, and I don't think there is any doubt that you thoroughly deserve to be in such a position. We here feel that had we won the rubber with the tactics we employed it would have been a tragedy for cricket as a game. I am sorry you have had such criticism of throwing as grousing in the middle of a series is thoroughly bad form. As a matter of fact we opened the question of throwing with our umpires last March and the matter was reopened in September when they had not no-balled one single suspect altho' they admitted that there were some. We considered we had four or five suspects and the practice was getting worse. I have no doubt that we shall have a general tightening up of the law next summer.

Don replied with a criticism of May's captaincy: 'Trueman is bowling to one slip and five on the on, except when the ball is new. Lock bowls to five on-side to both left and right hand batsmen. Tyson at one stage had five on and no slip at all. Bailey's leg theory was so blatant that Burke asked him if he knew where the stumps were.' He then went on to appeal to Robbie, the one man whom he thought might have enough influence to finally bring an end to slow play and time-wasting by begging him: '*Please never* send us a team again which averages 5½ minutes for every over throughout a Test.' Turning to the problems of bowlers throwing he was less concerned: 'It's all very well to rant about throwers — both countries have them — no country wants them, but there are far more important problems affecting the well-being of cricket. Your umpires' admission that they have passed bowlers whose actions are suspect is one of the best acts of self-condemnation I've ever read.'

Throwing now figured large in the discussions of every cricket board in the world. In England it was discussed at length by the ACCC and the search began for a definition of a 'throw', with the first-class umpires agreeing to compile a list of bowlers with doubtful actions during the 1958 season. But Robbie's attention was turning that summer to preparations for an MCC tour of the West Indies during the coming winter, as he had accepted the invitation to go as tour manager.

Chapter Fourteen
Tour Manager and Law 26

England had recovered from the disasters of the last Ashes tour in Australia and come back to beat India 5-0 in the summer of 1959. Now they faced the much tougher prospect of a tour in the West Indies and MCC asked Robbie to go as manager. He knew this was going to be a tough assignment, not only because the previous tour in 1953/54 under the captaincy of Hutton had been unpopular, but also because the newly independent islands were now trying to forge a political and economic federation to match their cricket unity, with the racial issue just below the surface. These factors were creating tension throughout the Caribbean as they jostled for position: Robbie was determined that the tour should run smoothly both on and off the field.

The selectors decided to give Peter May a young squad of players, none over 29 years old. Six had never toured abroad before and the whole party appeared to be more likely to respond to firm and sensible direction. Even so, few people gave May's team more than the slimmest hope of winning and the party foregathered at Lord's on the eve of sailing to be stimulated by a farewell address from Harry Altham, president of MCC. Afterwards, there was a talk and demonstration in the Long Room about the circuit training which was going to be used twice daily during the voyage to improve fitness. It seems that Robbie's influence was already taking effect, although there was one absentee from the sessions as Ted Dexter, recovering from jaundice, was delighted to report: 'I was forbidden exercise and spent my time on my back in the sun. Tough luck!' Not an attitude likely to endear itself to his new manager. The party embarked at Avonmouth on one of the banana boats owned by Fyffe's, the three-year-old *T.S.S.Camito*. Returning without cargo, it rolled its way across the Atlantic, keeping most of the players suffering below deck, although a few were badgered by Robbie to undertake some exercise outside and David Allen remembers running up and down staircases expecting to be pitched overboard at any moment. They arrived in Barbados on 18 December. The streets were lined with cheering citizens as the party made its way to the Marine Hotel.

After three warm-up games the First Test began with Cowdrey and Pullar walking out to open the England innings and face a barrage of hostile and short fast bowling. It had been Robbie's idea to force an unwilling Cowdrey to move up the order from the start of the tour, recognising that with his very straight bat and limited back-lift he had much more time to play the faster bowling, and now it paid off with a first-wicket stand of 50 while taking the sting out of the West Indian attack. Weathering the storm,

England reached a very creditable 482 before the West Indies proceeded to take over three days and 239 overs to grind out 563 runs, thanks to a stand of 399 between Sobers (226) and Worrell (197), and the game dragged on to a disappointing draw. Robbie would like to have seen the West Indies try to make a more positive attempt to secure a result for the Bridgetown crowd which Jim Swanton heard him describe as 'the most knowledgeable, the most appreciative, and the most sporting he has ever come across'. Now it was time to move on to Trinidad and two games before the Second Test at Port of Spain. Thanks to some imaginative declarations MCC beat Trinidad in two matches, and Robbie was becoming more involved in the pre-match preparations. Swanton reported that 'MCC have been putting in practice of a rather more whole-hearted character than was the rule in Australia and South Africa, with Walter Robins helping in the nets, in conjunction with the captain.'

In front of a crowd of about 30,000 spectators, the biggest in West Indian history to attend a sporting event, the West Indies began their first innings on the third day of the Second Test 360 runs behind England with all ten wickets intact. When play resumed after the tea interval they had struggled to 98 for seven when Ramadhin called Charran Singh for a sharp single to cover and the return from Dexter went straight to the top of the stumps leaving Singh a yard short of his crease and immediately given out by the umpire. The decision was received with a roar of protest, then boos, and then a rain of bottles, beer cans and other refuse was thrown onto the field of play. May called his fielders close to the boundary back into the middle, but then hundreds of spectators spilled onto the ground and the situation had descended into a riot, so that he had to lead his players back to the pavilion flanked by a police escort. The Governor of Trinidad and Tobago, the Prime Minister, the president of the West Indies Cricket Board, and the legendary ex-player Learie Constantine, now a minister in the island government, all went out to try to calm the crowd without success and the ground had to be cleared by mounted police and other reinforcements. An announcement was made over the public address system that play was abandoned for the day and the players were taken back to the Queen's Park Hotel.

At the hotel that evening, Robbie, wearing the chocolate and pale-blue striped tie of the Queen's Park Club as a demonstration of solidarity, read out a statement:

> It has come to my notice that rumours are being circulated that MCC intend to discontinue the Test match and go back to England. Such a suggestion never entered any of our minds at all. We intend to go on with the game. Our sympathies are entirely with the good people of Trinidad who have been let down by a few hooligans.

Later that night on Radio Trinidad, the Prime Minister, Dr Eric Williams read out the contents of a telegram he had sent to the MCC president in London apologising for the disruption of the Second Test. He went on to say: 'I understand that tomorrow the decision will be taken as to the future of this match. I can only express the hope, and I have reason to believe, that the decision will be in favour of continuation.' Alarmed by the suggestion that there was some doubt about the match being continued, Robbie called for a taxi and went straight round to see Sir Errol dos Santos, president of the West Indian Cricket Board, and not only obtained agreement that the match would definitely restart the following Monday but also negotiated extra time to be added to each of the last three days by starting half an hour earlier to make up for time lost by the disruption. The next day, Sunday 31 January, dos Santos arranged a conference in the Queen's Park Hotel attended by Robbie, Peter May and Colin Cowdrey; the committee of Queen's Park Cricket Club, which staged Test matches in Trinidad for the West Indies Board; Gerry Alexander, West Indies captain; and the Commissioner of Police, where the agreement was announced. Robbie repeated his sympathy for all the sportsmen of Trinidad and went on to say that his team firmly intended to return to Trinidad for the Fifth Test unless the West Indies Board should decide otherwise.

England went on to win the Test by 256 runs and then Robbie had a few comments to make which Swanton thought, although sound and true for all cricket, were

> specially appropriate in the context of a Test series in the West Indies. In brief, he reminded international cricketers that they are an example to all others: 'If they get into the habit of standing at the wicket when given out, it is not a good example. Neither is it protecting the umpires. The umpires do not want bodyguards, but they do want people to play the game in the right way.'

Swanton went on to say: 'If we never see a significant wait at the crease from now onwards, that will not be the least of Walter Robins' contribution to the success of the tour.'

The MCC party now moved on to Jamaica where they were comfortably lodged in chalets round a swimming pool in the garden of Courtleigh Manor Hotel and soon joined for a few days by various relatives — two wives, one father and mother, two fathers-in-law, a mother-in-law, a fiancée, and a special surprise for Robbie, his daughter, son-in-law and first grandchild. Ken Came had arranged leave from Kentucky, where he and Penny had been posted, so that they could bring Belinda for her christening, with Mrs Peter May as one of her godparents.

At this stage of the tour Swanton gave a short appraisal of how England were progressing: 'There are developments in this new England side which one is still waiting for, especially on the tactical side, where the approach sometimes is still strangely timid and unadventurous. Walter Robins must have cast his eyes to heaven more than once, for his own philosophy of cricket was so much more positive than that of this generation.'

On the sixth and final day of the Third Test at Sabina Park in Kingston, West Indies were 115 for four at tea, needing another 115 runs to win in 90 minutes. After another 30 minutes that target had been reduced to 85 and with Kanhai just reaching his half-century and well set, a shock victory looked possible. Then he suddenly went down with cramp and after a couple of minutes carried on in obvious discomfort. His partner and captain, Alexander, turned to May and asked for a runner but his request was refused although the England captain did call for a glass of water and a salt tablet for the suffering batsman. Alexander then went over to the square-leg umpire who conferred with the other umpire and the designated runner, Hunte, who had come on to the field was waved away. The game continued to a storm of booing and catcalls and some members of the press, sensing a front-page story, left their seats and made their way to the pavilion. Until he had the opportunity to discuss the incident with May at the end of play, Robbie had no intention of facing a barrage of questions from reporters and according to Cowdrey: 'He instructed the twelfth man to inform them that he could not be found and locked himself in the dressing-room lavatory.' Kanhai was soon out afterwards and the match ended with West Indies 55 runs short of victory and still four wickets in hand. Dismay and ill-feeling about May's refusal to allow Kanhai a runner continued for another half-hour after the players had left the field. After talking it over with Robbie, the England captain realised that Kanhai's cramp came under the heading of 'injury or illness' and that his consent to a runner was not required. From the start of the tour, Robbie had worked hard to know and help the Press corps and had earned their trust. He went over to the press box and explained that May had realized, on coming off the field, that his interpretation of the Law was at fault and that he had apologised to Kanhai and Alexander.

The MCC side which toured West Indies in 1959/60 winning the Test series 1-0. Standing (l to r): R.W.V.Robins (manager), K.F.Barrington, T.Greenhough, G.Pullar, A.E.Moss, R.Illingworth, D.A.Allen, K.V.Andrew (wk), R.Swetman (wk). Seated: E.R.Dexter, F.S.Trueman, M.C.Cowdrey, P.B.H.May (capt), J.B.Statham, M.J.K.Smith, R.Subba Row.

When Robbie arrived in Georgetown he heard that Peter May's wife had not returned to England as arranged but had re-joined her husband. Bearing in mind the criticism that May had received in Australia the previous winter for spending too much time with his then fiancée and too little with the team, Robbie expressed his surprise at the decision and asked him to think again. Other players' wives and fiancées had returned to England and it was thought that May should, for the last month of the tour, devote all his time and energies to the team. May refused to reconsider and Robbie had no powers to overrule him. Later that same day, May asked Robbie to come back and see him and expressed his concern at Robbie's attitude. Robbie had to emphasise that his responsibility lay with the interests of the team as a whole and during their argument, May went on to reveal that there was a special reason why he needed Virginia with him at that time. He was suffering discomfort and some bleeding from an internal abscess for which he had been operated on the previous July, and had secretly received attention from doctors in both Port-of-Spain and Kingston. Robbie was astounded that this information had been kept from him. It was obvious that, with Virginia due to arrive in a couple of days, the press would have another field-day. So Robbie decided that, to avoid speculation, the facts should be revealed. He took May to a doctor for an examination and on the last day of the match with British Guiana, went into the press box with a written statement. It said that, owing to the reopening of his operation wound, May had been advised by his doctor to rest for at least fourteen days, and that it was hoped that he would be fit for the Fifth Test.

Robbie immediately contacted Lord's to ask for MCC permission to arrange for Jim Parks, who was coaching in Trinidad, to join the squad but as there was not another room available in the team's hotel, Robbie was invited to stay with Peter Gibbings, managing director of a major local sugar and rum company. Just before Robbie transferred accommodation, Gibbings' wife had to leave on a trip to England and so Ian Peebles, who was covering the tour for the *Sunday Times*, was invited to join them. Peebles recalled the stay with some affection: 'We had a glorious ten days looked after by Bacchus, Peter's cricket-loving factotum, butler, and Jeeves. He was delighted to have Walter in the house, and countered the fearsome threats of what England was going to do to his side with spirited forecasts of sweeping victory.'

These events meant that Colin Cowdrey had to step up to take over the captaincy and being one match in front his approach was very clear: 'I had no intention of gambling away the chips Peter May had fought so courageously to win.' Sooner or later, this was bound to bring him into direct confrontation with Robbie and the tension between captain and manager deepened during the Fourth Test which dragged on after six days to another draw, thanks to slow batting by the West Indies and very defensive tactics on the part of Cowdrey. Brian Statham had been taking phone calls every day from his wife regarding his son, who was in hospital in Manchester. On the final afternoon Statham asked if he could leave and Robbie arranged for him to fly back home the next day. There was more bad news when Robbie was informed that May's wound had refused to heal in the hot climate and on the advice of his doctor he would be returning to England with his wife.

It was time for everyone to go back to Trinidad for the final Test. Now the arguments began. Without Statham and May, should England hang on to their one-game lead and adopt a defensive approach to avoid losing and therefore win the series? As far as Robbie was concerned every match was a match to be won and there was no other way to approach the game. When the match started it looked as if it was the West Indies who were aiming for a draw after Cowdrey had won the toss and elected to bat. By the end of play on the first day they had bowled no more than 75 overs. England on the other hand had played strokes from first to last and had reached 256 for three. Cowdrey was happy to report that 'Robins appeared to be quite pleased with our approach.' This would be the last time in the match that the actions of the England skipper would earn the approval of the manager.

Half an hour before the end of the fourth day, dilatory batting and bowling by each side had cancelled each other out when Alexander surprised everyone by deciding that it was time to look for victory. West Indies were still 55 runs behind England's first innings of 393 and with two wickets in hand, when Alexander declared the innings closed to give his bowlers half an hour to attack the England batting. The decision paid off when Cowdrey was caught by Worrell off Hall without scoring. England struggled on the fifth day to reach 168 for six at tea before Mike Smith and Jim Parks stopped the rot and added another 70 runs by end of play. Going into the last day 293 runs in front and with four wickets in hand seemed the perfect position for England to bat for about 30 minutes and go for some quick runs before declaring and setting West Indies a realistic target with a good chance of bowling them out if they accepted the challenge. This certainly was Robbie's choice. Peebles commented: 'Walter, characteristically, wanted to declare early and make a game of it.' That evening he 'made his views clear with his customary force.'

Parks and Smith did score quickly on the last morning and soon the question of a declaration needed to be considered if Robbie's wishes were going to be granted. But he wasn't there to argue his case. Urgent business matters had detained him at the hotel and in his absence Cowdrey turned to Peebles for advice on how Robbie would react if his very clear expectations were ignored. Peebles pointed out that if the positions were reversed, the West Indies would certainly not contemplate taking such a risk and that, as much as Robbie might disapprove, he would eventually understand why England had continued batting until they were in no danger of defeat. Cowdrey's idea of being out of danger meant batting on after lunch, delaying his declaration until Parks had completed his maiden Test century, and then giving the West Indies the impossible task of making 406 in 140 minutes.

When Robbie arrived early in the afternoon to discover what had taken place he was furious and entered the England dressing-room and rebuked Cowdrey in front of all those present before dissociating himself from the whole proceedings. Fortunately, Peebles was present to take care of his friend:

> He was much troubled by high blood pressure at this moment and easily upset, and I was much concerned for him. Knowing him so well I felt I could help, so I asked him to come and have a walk with me, at which we spent about twenty minutes pacing up and down behind the stand. I repeated my arguments, and said that he had himself been largely responsible for the tremendous success of the trip, and it would be foolish and unnecessary to throw away the victory which would crown their efforts, the more so as it was against long odds when they had set out. All this gave him time to breathe, and presently I was able to tell him to take a couple of his pills and rejoice, which he did.

Swanton ended his story of the tour with a few words about Robbie's management skills: 'The modern tour by an MCC team needs in its management a combination of strong discipline, cricket knowledge and background, and a sense of the importance of Press (i.e. public) relations. Walter Robins had a liberal supply of all three of these attributes.' *Wisden* later recorded: 'Under the wise management of R.W.V.Robins, the players developed a tremendous spirit and team-work and determination to avoid defeat carried them through to their triumph.' And one player in particular was more than happy with his methods:

> When touring abroad it is very important that the captain and the manager are in agreement and get on with each other because they are the most important of the personalities, the manager in particular. The first thing the manager has got to do, is to gain the confidence of his players and very quickly care about their welfare. I toured on four different occasions, twice to the West Indies and twice to Australia, and I would say without hesitation that a man called R.W.V.Robins, a man a lot of players didn't seem to like, was quite easily the best manager. You could talk to him, you could put your grievances to him and he was a willing listener. In fact he used to come to my bedroom every morning, sit in a chair and talk to me for at least half-an-hour about the conditions, and what we were trying to do and what we weren't trying to do that day.

That player was Freddie Trueman.

Trueman headed the Test bowling averages during the 1959/60 tour of the West Indies, taking twice as many wickets, 21, as the next highest wicket-taker, Statham, and bowling more overs than any other bowler. He also headed the bowling averages for all first-class games on the tour, took the most wickets, 37, and, apart from Illingworth, bowled the most overs. It seems that Robbie's special attention to the team's main strike bowler paid dividends.

* * * * * * *

In 1959, Robbie attended the annual Imperial Cricket Conference in London, as joint Australian delegate with Ben Barnett, the pre-war Australian Test wicketkeeper who had settled in England and was a close friend of the Robins family. After the meeting Robbie had written to

Bradman concerning the problems of bowlers with suspicious actions:

> It's a pity you or some other responsible member of your Board did not attend the Conference in July. As it was, Ben and I struggled through rather uncomfortably, neither of us being in a position to discuss throwing from the Australian angle. We had seen the film of some of your bowlers in Australia, and I was very disturbed when I saw it. I am enclosing a confidential report on Law 26. It will have been sent to your Board, but I would hate your NSW members to know you have had a preview prior to your meeting in September so destroy it when you have digested it.

However, the Australian Board of Control [ABC] preferred to try out their own version of Law 26 during their 1959/60 season which was unacceptable to MCC, and in 1959 MCC tried out one that was unacceptable in Australia.

In the summer of 1960 Bradman and the ABC were concerned that the Australian tour of England in 1961 would be disrupted by controversy if an amendment to Law 26 could not be agreed in advance, and Australia brought with them any of the bowlers whose action was under suspicion. The visitors to England in 1960 were South Africa and alarm bells sounded for Bradman when he heard that the main talking point was the bowling of Griffin who would eventually be no-balled at Lord's for throwing and not bowl again for the rest of the tour. Bradman decided to fly to London with Bill Dowling, Chairman of ABC, for the next meeting of the ICC scheduled for two days in July. At the start of the meeting, according to R.S.Rait Kerr, 'Mr Altham offered a solemn undertaking on behalf of MCC, that England would exclude from international teams and tours all bowlers whose actions were considered suspect.' Bradman, Dowling and the West Indies delegates were not happy to commit their Boards to a similar policy 'on the grounds that not to select a bowler would be to take authority away out of the hands of the umpire and that selectors would be in an impossible position if they undermined respect for their own umpires by failing to select bowlers whom they had passed as fair.' Nevertheless, the countries reaffirmed unanimously their determination to eradicate throwing from cricket and during the meeting they reached agreement to rephrase Law 26:

> A ball shall be deemed to have been thrown if, in the opinion of either umpire, the bowling arm, having been bent at the elbow, whether the wrist is backward of the elbow or not, is suddenly straightened prior to the instant of delivery. The bowler shall nevertheless be at liberty to use the wrist freely in the delivery action.

During his flight back to Australia Don composed a letter to Robbie:

> I am sorry time did not permit another meeting before I left for Australia but you will remember almost your last remark to me was: 'if you can bring about peace between England and Australia for the 1961 tour, it will have been your greatest innings.' Well, I think I have done it, PROVIDING YOU will really get behind a proposal which I have put forward, details which will reach you from Harry [Altham] and Gubby and MCC, but I beg of you not to allow any narrow-minded pinpricking members of MCC to block the proposal on the score of suspicion. If

they don't place any faith in our sincerity and want to rule cricket from an ivory tower, let them say so and get on with it. I know who would regret it most. I'm sure my idea will work and it will do so without loss of face by either side.

Bradman's proposal was that, at the start of the 1961 tour, there should be a moratorium over the throwing question until the eve of the First Test, and that no umpire should call an Australian bowler during matches before then, but that the Test match umpires should have an early opportunity of seeing them and sending a confidential report to the MCC president on any bowler whose action they thought was suspect. By the time Bradman's letter arrived, Robbie had been advised of the details of his proposal and he immediately replied by cable: 'Your letter just received. Peebles and self in full agreement. I shall argue your case exactly as stated. Peebles thinks good hope of success. Please regard confidential. Regards to all from us both.'

Before knowing MCC's decision, Bradman wrote to Robbie again:
You've no idea of the feeling in this country. The press have branded England as 'squealers' in headlines right across the page, some writers openly accuse MCC of forcing the English umpires to call Griffin and certain English bowlers as a red-herring to make sure they do the same to Meckiff or Burke, or to frighten Australia into not selecting them for the Tour. You haven't got any problems over there — you ought to be here and try and get any support. I'd need a bodyguard if I said to a Sydney chap that Rorke throws.

MCC accepted Bradman's proposal but with the proviso that, when the moratorium ended, umpires were instructed to 'call' bowlers on the field and, to avoid inequality, the counties would agree to extend the moratorium to English bowlers in matches against the touring Australians. As a result the plans for the forthcoming tour went ahead and Don wrote to Robbie: 'It is good to have this agreement between MCC and ourselves settled, and, all in all, I think it has had a pretty good reception from the press.'

Soon after his arrival back in Australia, Bradman was elected chairman of the ABC. That season Australia awaited the arrival of the West Indies team with rather more than the usual anticipation for a Test series. Each captain, Frank Worrell for the visitors and Richie Benaud for Australia, were known to be determined to play the game as it should be played, with lively enjoyment. Even so, on the night before the first Test began in Brisbane, Bradman felt compelled to ask if he could address the Australian team. He told the players that the selectors, of which he was the unofficial chairman, would be predisposed towards individuals who played attractive, winning cricket — those who pulled in the crowds. That game ended with the teams tied in what many consider the most exciting finish ever to a Test match and after that, as Roland Perry has written, 'crowds came back to the Tests in their tens of thousands. In the next Test match at Melbourne a world record of 90,800 people came through the gates on the Saturday. The series, which the home team won, was probably the most sensational ever played in Australia.' The last Test ended on 15

February 1961 and Bradman wrote to Robbie:

> We have just concluded the most pleasant and exciting Test series I have ever seen, or ever expect to see. The cricket was bright and entertaining and the players had personality. There was a spirit between the teams which surmounted, at all times, the hard knocks that were given and taken, and everyone seemed to realise that they were there to entertain the public as well as to try to win matches!

When it came to selecting the Australian team to tour England in the summer of 1961, none of the bowlers with doubtful actions were chosen, mainly due to their loss of form rather than any reluctance of the selectors, and the Test series continued without controversy. Australia played attractive cricket to retain the Ashes by winning 2-1, but England had chances at least to square the series, particularly in the Fourth Test at Old Trafford. And, according to Dexter, the reason why England lost that Test was interference from Robbie at a crucial moment of the game! At tea on the third day, England were 168 runs ahead with four wickets in hand and Barrington 78 not out, when Dexter says Robbie entered the dressing-room and 'insisted that we should get on with it'. When the game resumed, Barrington was immediately out caught off Simpson and the next three wickets fell quickly to give England a lead of only 177. Australia came back strongly and left England to make 255 to win which proved to be 54 runs too many. Dexter doesn't explain why Barrington, or any of the other England players, should have paid attention to Robbie as he was not a selector and May, England's captain, would have over-ruled any rash change of tactics. It is even possible that Robbie was not in Manchester at any time during that Test match as he was certainly over 200 miles away on the south coast the following Tuesday. Richard Robins remembers that 'RWV was with my pals and I in Portsmouth watching Middlesex playing Hampshire on that fateful last day! I can remember him saying, as we listened to the radio at the ground and the wickets started tumbling, to Benaud, "Poor old Gubby must be speechless!"'

Robbie had other important matters to deal with that summer. An Enquiry Committee should have sat in the spring of 1961, but owing to the death of R.S.Rait Kerr, who was to have been chairman, it was postponed until the autumn. In the meantime a small sub-committee under Robbie's chairmanship was selected to examine all possible alternative structures for the game, in the light of continually falling attendance at championship matches. In May, Robbie wrote to Bradman: 'Despite the promise of the captains, county cricket remains slow and dull. These young professionals are cutting their own throats. Everyone seems to be more engrossed in technique than the cricket and how it should be presented to the public.' Bradman replied: 'I loved your phrase about players being more engrossed in technique than cricket. I have preached that sentiment for donkey's years. In the long run it all gets back to the old story that it doesn't matter where the feet are, what matters is where the ball goes.' Throughout the summer the sub-committee continued their investigations and 'under Mr Robins' energetic guidance, considered numerous permutations and prepared a report for the enquiry committee when it was convened again in the autumn with Sir Hubert Ashton in the chair.' That report was placed before the counties in December who vetoed any experiments taking place in 1962, but agreed to cut the number of championship matches to 28 and introduce a knock-out competition in 1963.

Chapter Fifteen
Chairman of England Selectors

At the end of the 1961 season Gubby Allen decided to step down as Selection Committee chairman and Robbie took his place. Soon after the appointment was confirmed Robbie received a letter from Bradman:

> I can assure you the appointment carries the approbation of all Australians, especially me, and although it does not lend itself to co-operation in that you have to pick a team to beat us (and I the same in reverse). I feel certain we shall find ways and means of working together in the interests of the game as a whole. You know you carry my whole-hearted respect and admiration and we'll always be able to talk man-to-man.

Robbie was joined by two newcomers to the role of selector, Alec Bedser and Willie Watson, plus Doug Insole for a fourth consecutive year. Robbie felt it was necessary to explain to Insole exactly how he thought the new Selection Committee should operate under his guidance as chairman, and hoping that he could rely upon his support, he immediately wrote to him:

> I hope you will not think I am rushing my fences if I put on paper thoughts I have on what should be our approach to cricket by the England side this summer and during next winter in Australia. If you do not agree, remember that I, too, only have one vote.

> A tremendous responsibility rests on English cricket — in terms of our approach to the game — in Australia next winter. Australia have recently enjoyed a remarkable series with West Indies. Unfortunately for us they contrast West Indian with English cricket as they have seen it on tours since the war, and we haven't shown them much. I can't get that 106 runs in a day at Brisbane out of mind. Anything that is done to lessen the importance and appreciation of matches between the two countries is, I feel, a nail in the coffin of cricket as we would wish it to be. It is vital that we show the cricketing world that English cricketers appreciate what is required in Test cricket in this day and age. The first essential is that the Selection Committee demonstrate their approval of attacking cricket. Some of our cricketers are not prepared to take a chance, if by doing so, they run the risk of failure. Both team and individual should be prepared to take chances. I think it wins more matches and catches the imagination of the public. This should be made quite clear to captain and team. We must insist on quality before quantity in the county cricketer's game. One remembers how a series was played rather than who won it, the team and captain must be convinced that if they lose it is not a national disaster. This has been my personal experience. I would appoint a captain for one

match at a time, and if he failed us I would drop him. Players must be given instructions before going out to bat. Selfishness is at the bottom of some of the trouble, and players must be told that this, we will not tolerate; we may not get very far with some, but if they get into their heads that what we want we are halfway. Players must be made to be enthusiastic and enjoy themselves. Spectators are quick to appreciate enthusiasm and for this reason alone it is worth insisting upon, whether it is naturally present or not. I hope you will forgive my frankness, it's because I feel so desperately anxious for the success of our next tour to Australia. We have a job to do this summer against Pakistan for our stock is low and our chances of winning in Australia to say the least, dubious. All things being equal I think our main chance is to grasp the nettle.

Insole voiced no disagreement with Robbie's revolutionary proposals and at a press conference at Lord's the new chairman issued a solemn pledge that the selectors would give priority to players of enterprise and courage. He went on to affirm that there would be no place whatsoever for defensive techniques in the teams they chose to represent England. He then expressed a personal view that emphasised just how serious he was taking this new policy: 'I would not mind losing all five Tests in Australia if we played the right way!' Not surprisingly, that was a step too far for many and Robbie clarified his approach: 'I play to win and try to win from the word go. I play to draw only if I feel we may lose. I loathe losing; the hardest job I ever had as captain was to walk into the opponent's dressing-room with a set grin on my face and congratulate the winner.'

Pakistan were the visitors that summer and unlikely to present much of a challenge, so the main interest lay in the selection of the side for Australia the following winter, with special emphasis on the choice of captain. Peter May had retired from Test cricket and Colin Cowdrey saw himself as his natural successor although he had temporarily put himself out of the picture by preferring not to take the MCC side on the tour of Pakistan and India the previous winter. Ted Dexter had stepped in but the results had been disappointing, with England losing two and drawing five of the last seven Tests which had featured negative play of the most depressing kind from all three teams. Some members of the press were concerned that neither Dexter nor Cowdrey was capable of leading a team with the right creativity that could bring back the Ashes and that the selectors should look elsewhere. E.M.Wellings of the London *Evening News* had the idea that David Sheppard might be interested and in a brief interview put it to him that it was desperately important for English cricket that he should go to Australia on the next tour as captain as he was precisely the type of leader urgently need to restore vitality to England's Test team. Flattered by the suggestion, Sheppard said that he was intending to take a long leave soon, and that it was a possibility that he might be available for Australia, but that he had not been officially approached on the matter. There are several versions of what happened next. What is clear, however, is that Robbie, like Puck the mischievous servant of Oberon in 'Midsummer Night's Dream, led everyone a merry dance as he orchestrated the return of Sheppard to keep the gentlemen of the press on their toes for what they saw as the biggest cricket story to come their way for years, 'Man of God Leads England to Recover Holy Grail', while keeping everyone guessing by bringing first Dexter, then Cowdrey, on to the stage as his leading man.

After the interview was published, Robbie took immediate action and telephoned the Mayflower Centre, at Canning Town in East London, where Sheppard was based, to find out if he was serious about returning to first-class cricket. Unfortunately, Sheppard was not in his office at the time but Robbie left a message with his secretary. By an unfortunate coincidence, Sheppard had a parishioner also with the surname Robins who sometimes telephoned him and wanted to talk at length about something that had already taken up a great deal of the Reverend's time, and not wishing to become involved again at the expense of other members of his parish, Sheppard asked his secretary to put the message to one side to be followed up at a more convenient time. A week later he remembered the message and when she said that she believed the caller had been Robbie, he telephoned him immediately and Robbie told him: 'If it's true that you are available for this tour, it's the best news I've heard for English cricket for a long time.' It was agreed that Sheppard should start playing as soon as possible so that he and the selectors could review his fitness and form. Sheppard said that 'I would play two months cricket for Sussex and that I would be available for the tour of Australia in any capacity. The possibility of the captaincy had been mentioned to me, but I made no assumption in that direction.' That didn't stop the press from drawing their own conclusions about what they thought was now a three-way competition between Dexter, Cowdrey and Sheppard.

Once the series began against Pakistan, Dexter continued as captain, but after two easy victories, Robbie and his committee decided to shake everyone up and promote Cowdrey above his rival for the Third Test at Leeds which was soon won by an innings. Cowdrey may well have held on to the captaincy for the last two Tests and then taken the side to Australia, but there was to be another twist to the story when illness prevented him from playing at Lord's as captain of the Gentlemen against the Players and Dexter replaced him. Before then, Sheppard had begun his return in grand style with a century against Oxford University, but it was a different matter once he returned to the higher level of county cricket and he struggled. In the next 12 innings he scored 297 runs at an average of 27.00 with a highest score of 95 against Northamptonshire. Even so, the press entourage had followed him avidly, recording his every run. After his sixth game for Sussex, against Surrey at The Oval, Sheppard went over to Lord's to meet Robbie and Gubby Allen and told them: 'It was an intriguing idea but I haven't done as well as I had hoped. It has not been easy coming back after so long a lay-off. My batting hasn't been quite what I had expected and I found the fielding rather difficult. Perhaps we'd better forget the whole thing.' Robbie persuaded him to persevere and that they should talk again after his next match, which would be the Gentlemen versus Players at Lord's, during which the appointment of the captain for Australia would be confirmed.

The press now assembled at Lord's in force, convinced that it was a straight fight between Sheppard and Dexter, both of Sussex. Sheppard scored 112 in the first innings and everyone was sure that this had swung the captaincy his way. From the windows of the press restaurant a number of journalists spotted Robbie walking back to the pavilion. Hoping that they would get advance notice that Sheppard was the man, they desperately tried to attract his attention by a series of long-range hand signals. Robbie seized the opportunity for one more piece of mischief and gave them the thumbs-up, fooling them into believing that they had been right all along and that he and his fellow selectors were going to choose the man the press were certain he had wanted from the start. They rushed back to their typewriters to compose their stories for the following morning with headlines proclaiming 'Sheppard for Captain'. Later that day came the announcement to a stunned press box that Dexter had been appointed England's captain for the tour of Australia, with Cowdrey as vice-captain. In their desperation for a good story, the press had not realised that Robbie had been ringing the changes and introducing red herrings like Sheppard only to satisfy himself that, in Dexter, he had the right man with the right attitude to challenge Richie Benaud in a battle of wills in the Test arena in Australia.

Sheppard honoured his promise to go on the tour, whether as captain or not, and did well although the series was drawn 1-1. *Wisden* later reported that England had not regained the Ashes and 'much of the cricket in the five Tests in the Antipodes fell below expectations. Too much emphasis was put on avoiding defeat in preference to thinking in terms of victory from the very first ball.' This was exactly the type of cricket that Robbie thought he had ensured would not happen when he chose Dexter as captain, although Dexter himself, when at the crease, had showed more ambition than most batsmen on either side. Perhaps if Robbie had been there personally for the last two Tests in the New Year at Adelaide and Sydney as he had planned, when there was still a chance to bring back the Ashes, he may have been able to inspire England to believe that it was better to lose 3-1 while trying to win 3-1, than settling for no more defeats and a drawn series. Tragically, his father had become seriously ill just when Robbie was due to fly to Australia and he had cancelled his trip. Vivian passed away two weeks later at the age of 82.

*　*　*　*　*　*　*

It was back to business as usual for Robbie after the England team returned from the 1962/63 tour of Australia and New Zealand. The visitors in the summer of 1963 were the West Indies and it was hoped that the almost unchanged West Indies team from the great series of 1960/61 in Australia would revitalise Test cricket in England and bring back missing crowds.

But first there was an MCC conference in April arranged by the special LBW Sub-committee, with Gubby Allen as chairman, to hear the case for reverting to the old law which, it was suggested, would bring the line of play more to the off-side and encourage attacking cricket. It was agreed that there should be no reversion to the old lbw law without a widening of the wicket and that net trials should be conducted and a trial match played in July with a four-stump wicket measuring eleven inches wide. Robbie wrote to Bradman: 'I did not turn up at the lbw meeting last week as I am much against any change and really I am fed up with the numerous changes which have been tried over the last ten years, including the front foot.' Bradman agreed:

> Regarding the lbw law, I'm afraid I cannot see the logic of those who want to go back to the pre-1935 law. It had failed and people felt impelled to change it. If not, they wouldn't have done so. Why did it fail? Mainly because people like Sutcliffe shouldered arms and refused to play shots at balls outside the off stump. The new 1935 law was designed to force them to play at such balls. I see no evidence whatever that a return to the old law will cause fellows like Cowdrey and Barrington to alter their style. I played under both laws, it didn't alter my method of play at all. Perhaps the new law has encouraged negative forward play, bat and pad. Here I think umpires have tended to overdo giving the man not out if he played forward, thus encouraging him to play forward negatively. If I could be persuaded that batsmen would play more shots if we went back to the old law, I might listen, but I can't see it. I am aware that some fellows, like Cowdrey, today ostensibly play at the ball, but in fact deliberately play outside it, with the pad inside to intercept the ball. I believe it is simple to tell the genuine from the phoney. And this business of bat over shoulder and pads in front, should have gone out with horse trams. But all in all, your philosophy is right. Players must have the right mental approach to hit the ball à la Sobers. If they did, grounds would be full, I would fly 1,000 miles to see him bat tomorrow, but I wouldn't go across the road to watch some of our so-called batsmen. That would be the position under any rules whatever.

When July came, nothing positive had been learned from the net trials and players in the experimental match showed little enthusiasm. The Committee reported back the pros and cons and MCC recommended to the ACCC that no immediate change should be made. Perhaps Robbie had been right not to waste his time by being involved.

Despite the England's poor showing in Australia the selectors decided to keep Dexter as captain, hoping that he would respond to the leadership style of Frank Worrell, the West Indian skipper. In the First Test, at Old Trafford, Worrell gave a clear indication of how he intended his team to always look for victory when he declared the West Indies first innings closed as soon as they reached 500 on the afternoon of the second day, instead of the usual international captain's policy of batting on to build a score that ensured they could not be beaten. It paid off and England were forced to follow on and lost by ten wickets with a day to spare. Robbie wrote to Bradman: 'Frank Worrell is not only a splendid person and a fine character but a great leader and his team rightly will do anything for him.' It was obviously going to be a series that was guaranteed to give Robbie enormous pleasure and restore his faith in Test cricket and he confided in Bradman: 'If it happens that we get beaten at Lord's there will be the old cry of "sack the selectors" but I couldn't care less providing the same type of cricket is played.'

The Lord's Test was a tremendous match from start to finish, one of the greatest of all time. For five days both sides were convinced that they were going to win and it all came down to the last two balls from the last over. England needed six runs to win with their last two batsmen at the wicket although Cowdrey at the bowler's end had his left arm in plaster after suffering a broken wrist and would bat left-handed if necessary. Every known result of a finished cricket match was possible. When the game ended everyone agreed that it was the most exciting draw they had ever witnessed. Robbie wrote again to Bradman saying: 'The Lord's Test was the best game I have ever seen, although the weather was atrocious, you will never see a better innings than Dexter's.' England won the Third Test by 217 runs, thanks to the bowling of Fred Trueman who followed his 11 wickets at Lord's with 12 at Edgbaston, including taking his last six wickets for only four runs in a 24-ball spell. Robbie wrote: We owe our success entirely to Freddie Trueman who bowled magnificently in the last innings. Typical of Freddie, when I congratulated him he said, 'Thank you, Mr Chairman — I did it for you and for England.'

At Leeds the West Indies re-asserted their superiority to go 2-1 up in the series, and went on to take the Wisden Trophy in its inaugural year with an eight-wicket victory in the last Test. Robbie had nothing but praise for the winners: 'Well, we had another wonderful exhibition of how the game should be played by the West Indians in the Fifth Test.' After the series was over, Robbie received a letter from Frank Worrell: 'I would like to take this opportunity to thank you for your welcome contribution and assistance to us on our tour. We return to the Caribbean proud men, proud at the thought of having assisted the counties and England elevens in providing the spectators with the sort of cricket they desired.' But some people believed that Griffith, the West Indies fast-bowler, had taken 33 wickets using a doubtful bowling action which tainted their success although Robbie wrote to Bradman after the series: 'it is a funny thing that this question of chucking was never mentioned in my presence in Selection Committees or in the dressing-room. I did hear a lot of muttering in various Committee rooms around the country, but as most of the remarks were from people who couldn't see a googly out of the hand or in the air, I didn't take very much notice.'

Doug Insole, who had continued as a member of Robbie's selection committee, also wrote to him in characteristic tones:

> It has indeed been a pleasure, a privilege, and quite a bit of fun, to have served under your gentle guidance. We may not have stuffed 'em, but at least the customers had some pretty useful stuff to watch, and the heroic British press have seized on the fact that we bowled and batted quicker than the opposition — at least part object of the exercise. Anyway, whether or not we get thrown together again next season, I reckon we have jointly made very nearly the best of a fairly difficult job, which is not particularly modest, but then, what the hell!

The England selectors meeting in the Robins 'dining room' in Hall Gate near Lord's. Left to right; Alec Bedser, Willie Watson, Robbie (chairman), Doug Insole and Ted Dexter.

Hope you are installed at Hall Road, and your efforts have received the appreciation they deserve.

Insole had mentioned Hall Road and this was a reference to Robbie's new residence in London since August. Robbie had been deeply affected by the death of his father at the beginning of the year, not only because he would no longer be seeing him at his desk in the offices of the family business, but because Vivian had lived with the family in Hampshire for the past seven years. He and Robbie had spent many hours together working in the garden and grounds, as well as fishing side-by-side in the river which Vivian had stocked with young trout, going off to play the occasional game of cricket or to watch Charles or Richard in school and university matches. Robbie, now 57, decided it was time for the family to leave Froyle and move into a smaller, easier-to-manage home. Penelope and Charles were now both married and had their own homes. Richard had decided not to go on from Eton to university and had arranged to move to Australia in September to train as a journalist, so there was only Unity, still at school, who would need to move with them. They found the ideal new home at 2 Hall Gate, a small neo-Georgian terraced house in St John's Wood with a view of Lord's from the bedroom window. He was delighted with the change and, according to Kathleen, 'he was in his element wandering about Lord's, whether there was cricket or not, talking to the staff and the young pros, and attending all the committees, and in the evenings he would play real tennis at which, with his usual enthusiasm, he became very proficient.' As an administrator he could be unpredictable according to John Warr: 'I remember him as chairman of a Middlesex committee reading out an apology for his own absence. When he was chided about it he replied that he had turned up because he realised that he could not

127

trust us to make the right decision.'

Soon after moving to St John's Wood, the final of the new one-day knock-out competition was held at Lord's before a capacity crowd, 'cheering on their favourites and flaunting banners and coloured rosettes as if they were at Wembley.' At long last, one of Robbie's dreams for the future of cricket was had been realised. Robbie's last responsibility as chairman of the selectors that year was to put together a team for the MCC winter tour of India, reduced to only ten matches but still containing five Tests. All eyes turned to the arrival in England of the latest Australian tourists and the expectation of another thrilling Test series like the West Indian tour twelve months earlier.

But before the Test series got underway, Robbie made one more visit to Eton College with another team from the Forty Club. Since 1950, he had captained a team almost every year at the start of the season, taking with him numerous volunteers as keen as himself to encourage schoolboy cricket, including such great players, by then retired, as both the Compton brothers, Denis and Leslie; both Bedser twins, Alec and Eric; Godfrey Evans and Laurie Fishlock; ex-England captains George Mann and Freddy Brown; the Australians Keith Miller, Ben Barnett and Arthur Morris; New Zealander Martin Donnelly; as well as friends Ian Peebles and Jim Swanton.

When the Test matches did start, with Dexter back at the helm for England, they were frequently affected by bad weather and never lived up to expectations. It was much the same old story — slow play, negative bowling, defensive fields, and time wasting. When the two teams met at Old Trafford for the Fourth Test, Simpson, the Australian captain, had only one result in mind. If this Test was drawn, Australia would retain the Ashes, even if England went on to win at The Oval. As far as he was concerned, nothing else mattered. It was the negation of everything that Robbie believed cricket, at any level, should aspire to. Winning the toss, Simpson opened the innings on Thursday morning, 23 July, and was still batting 12 hours and 40 minutes later before he was out for 311 at 646 for six on Saturday afternoon. When England started batting, with only a draw to play for, they were equally dour and Barrington responded with 256 in eleven hours and 23 minutes, while Dexter took eight hours for his 174. A saddened Robbie wrote to Bradman: 'I was not enamoured of the cricket at Old Trafford and, in fact, on the Friday afternoon I crept out and went to the cinema.'

There was another draw at The Oval so Simpson could also claim to having won the series although this failed to impress Robbie who wrote to Bradman: 'I will make no comment on the cricket because although affected by bad weather it was the dullest series I have ever seen between England and Australia.' Earlier, Robbie and his committee had chosen the side to go on the MCC tour to South Africa that winter. They beat the South Africans 1-0, so Robbie's period as chairman ended on a positive note, as he had decided to resign. When Bradman heard the news, he wrote immediately to express his regret and Robbie replied: 'You say you are sorry that I have given up the chairmanship but I had to, because I was so very disappointed with the series this year compared with that against the West Indies in 1963.' In response to a letter from Warwickshire County Cricket Club also expressing regret at his decision, Robbie summed it all up: 'I quit because I wasn't amused, it's as simple as that.'

Chapter Sixteen
Final Years

In 1965 rumours began to circulate that there had been 'instructions from Lord's' to umpires to turn a blind eye to the bowling action of Charlie Griffith during the 1963 tour, and again in 1964 when he came to England as a member of a West Indian team led by Sir Frank Worrell to play three exhibition matches at Scarborough, Edgbaston and Lord's in September. Eventually the MCC Committee issued a statement denying all knowledge that any 'influential member' of MCC had advised the first-class umpires not to call Griffith, backing the statement with a categorical denial from each umpire on the first-class list that anyone had been so approached.

Despite that denial, rumours persisted and some years later, Robbie was dragged in to the story as one of the suspected conspirators who had ensured that Griffith would continue to bowl with his action unchallenged. In his autobiography, *Ball of Fire*, published in 1977, Freddie Trueman wrote that, when England were due to bat during the Second Test in 1963:

> I was having a quiet soak in one of the individual bathrooms at Lord's. The place was otherwise deserted. Then I heard voices in the corridor outside. And I found myself listening to R.W.V.Robins, chairman of the England selectors at the time, apparently talking to the two umpires about the suspect action of Griffith and the complaints which had been coming in from various counties. I heard him say that the umpires should under no circumstances call Griffith for throwing. When they objected he explained that there was a lot of worry about racial tension in London and he feared a riot might be sparked off if Griffith was no-balled. When I came out of the bathroom Mr Robins was waiting for me. He had heard me moving about. He asked me if I had overheard the conversation so I had to admit that indeed I had. Then he solemnly asked me to give my word never to disclose it. I promised I would keep silent for a time but told him that I thought it should be made public eventually if only to point out the handicap England had been playing under. I must say I was amazed that the chairman of selectors could give such guidance to umpires.

Analysis of the possible time-scale, purpose and location of those conversations, as presented by Trueman, suggest that 'the who, where, when, what and why' of his account were pure invention. He would have been taking his bath either at the end of the first day's play or during the morning of the second day when West Indies had been dismissed for 301. Whichever moment it was, we are asked to believe that Robbie took the opportunity of a chance encounter, or deliberately sought out the umpires, to discuss an extremely secret matter in the corridor outside the England dressing-rooms and bathrooms, a location where other players would be going back and forth at irregular intervals and where there was no reason for the umpires to be present as their changing-room was at the other end of the pavilion, behind the visitors' dressing-room. If it happened on the second day between the change of innings, the only opportunity to buttonhole the umpires and give them specific instructions before they returned to the field, would have to have been at their own dressing-room, far from where Trueman was taking his bath.

If the story as told by Trueman did not happen, why would he invent it? When it came to write his autobiography it must have seemed an opportunity to put the record straight regarding the lack of support he believed that he and other players should have received from the cricket authorities on various occasions during his career. In particular, it must have rankled that despite his heroic efforts taking 34 wickets in the 1963 series, England had lost 3-1, mainly due to what some believed was MCC allowing the West Indies to continue playing with a bowler with a suspect action who had taken 32 wickets. Robbie had passed away before Trueman's book was published, so was not available to deny the accusation. When composing the story, who would be better to pick out as the leading actor in the scenario than good old Robbie, with his reputation for being a bit of a loose cannon. Perhaps that is why the location of the conversation has definite echoes of the altercation 33 years before, when Shrimp Leveson Gower had sought out Robbie for a dressing down and a very public exchange of views was acted out on the landing outside the England dressing-room. Trueman does try to excuse Robbie's behaviour by suggesting that Robbie was acting with the best of intentions in the interest of racial harmony, and then goes even further to embellish his story by saying that, when they met two years later, Robbie told him it was the best-kept secret in cricket, which would not have been very difficult as there was no secret to keep.

* * * * * * *

Returning to the events of 1965, Robbie played at Lord's that summer in a one-day match between Middlesex Past and Future and Surrey Past and Future when he was joined by old friends, Robertson, Dewes, Bedford and the Compton brothers. He scored a few runs before being bowled by Laker and even bowled a couple of overs himself, but without capturing any wickets to prevent Surrey winning in an exciting finish. He certainly had not yet decided to retire completely, and was continuing to keep himself active with real tennis and by joining the Bowls Club at Brondesbury Cricket Ground. He had also been going to Zermatt every winter with Ken Garcke to enter curling competitions, a sport he had taken up in the early 1960s. Kathleen and Unity went with them one year and Kathleen recalled that she was 'amazed at the great reception Ken and Walter got from the "regulars", mostly Scotsmen with whom they played (or curled) for those Challenge Cups.'

The ICC met as usual in July 1965 and attempted again to solve the problem of bowlers' illegal actions. They came up with an interim definition for consideration but this was not accepted by Australia and encouraged further discussion in England. In October, MCC appointed a special sub-committee under George Mann to advise on steps to be taken to eliminate throwing from all grades of cricket, and in the same month *The Cricketer* magazine published a four-page feature, 'Throwing: The Shadow on the Game', in which Robbie declared 'the bent arm "bowler" has no case for consideration, and his elimination would be in the best interests of all who conscientiously seek to observe the spirit as well as the letter of the law.'' The MCC sub-committee reached a conclusion in November and proposed the definition:

> A ball shall be deemed to have been thrown if, in the opinion of either Umpire, the bowling arm is straightened, whether partially or completely during that part of the action which immediately precedes the ball leaving the hand. This definition shall not debar the bowler from the use of the wrist in delivering the ball.

In the meantime, Kathleen and Unity went to Australia in October for six months holiday. Richard was still living and working there and he had found them a flat in Darling Point, a harbour-side suburb of Sydney. Robbie would join them after Christmas and, as England were touring there that winter, planned to see the last three Ashes Tests before returning with Kathleen and Unity to England. But Robbie was not in the best of health when he arrived. The cumulative effect of the stress he had endured during the Caribbean tour; the strain of three seasons as chairman of the selection committee; anxiety during Kathleen's recuperation from peritonitis following an appendix operation in 1962; then the deaths of his father and brother-in-law the following winter; the necessary but sad departure from Froyle; plus the responsibilities of being head of Stafford, Knight, the family business in the City; as well as recovering from a number of small strokes since the diagnosis of high blood pressure in 1957; had all contributed to his decline.

But his spirits were soon raised when, on the first morning of the Third Test in Sydney, he watched Boycott and Barber open England's innings with 234 runs in 240 minutes. England went on to win by an innings and go one-up in the series. His next big surprise came at Adelaide when, in reply to England's first innings of 241 he saw Simpson and Lawry open Australia's innings with a stand of 244 in only 266 minutes. With the series all-square when the teams arrived at Melbourne the scene was set for a dramatic finish. 'The captains promised that they would be "out to win"', according to John Woodcock in *The Cricketer*. England batted first and had reached 419 for seven by lunch on the second day, with the perfect opportunity to force the pace with the intention of declaring before the tea interval and capturing some Australian wickets before close of play. Instead, England played for safety while only adding another 66 runs in 90 minutes before declaring at 485 for nine. After losing their first two wickets, including Simpson for 36, the Australian batsmen saw no reason to take the risk of losing their hold on the Ashes and began to play for a draw. Lawry took over six hours to make 108 and Cowper used up 727 minutes to make 307 before Simpson finally declared at 543 for eight late in the afternoon of the final day. Robbie went home depressed that, despite all his efforts over the years, nothing had changed.

Later that summer the arguments over illegal bowling actions continued and at the ICC annual meeting in July, where Robbie and Ben Barnett again represented Australia, all the members accepted George Mann's committee definition for one year only, to begin in 1967. Bradman wrote to Robbie:

> You said you would write me after the ICC meeting but no letter to hand. I've seen Ben Barnett's report so I'll get in first. Apparently MCC, without answering the penetrating questions from Australia, was just determined to have her own way. The over-extended arm business was not submitted to other countries before the meeting and should never have been raised. Moreover, the wording is an open invitation to anyone who cares to throw, to do so and claim they are merely straightening an 'O/E' arm. Apparently Australia is now the only country prepared to take action. I'm fed up.

Robbie replied: 'At the moment, as I see it, there is no solution to this terrible problem, so it's back to the admin boys who are doing everything in their power, just as Australia has done for the past four years. I attended the ICC in July and hardly said a word.' Due to the decline in his health, this would be Robbie's last handwritten letter to his friend.

In 1966 Robbie played his last game at Lord's, appearing for the Cross Arrows against the Middlesex Young Amateurs on the Nursery Ground in September. Richard had returned from Australia:

> I had the great good fortune to play under his captaincy in that last match. Although clearly unwell [he had virtually lost the use of his left hand — perhaps Parkinson's] he took the captaincy and put the Middlesex team in first and got me on to bowl early. They couldn't read me at all and were bundled out for 120. We opened up with two young men who went on to play county cricket, and by mid afternoon were cruising to a ten-wicket victory. To the astonishment of the two young batting pros, at 60 for none there was a loud clapping from the boundary as RWV called them in and declared — in a one innings match! He invited the Young Amateurs to go in again and set a target and during their second innings their opener sent a skier to RWV at deep mid-off which he caught one handed, shielding his weak left hand. The Young Amateurs declared leaving the Cross Arrows to get 120 in 75 minutes and we got them in the last over in front of an excited crowd. When I went over to applaud one of the openers after the game, he said: 'What a stupid thing to do. We could all have gone home early!' A typical response from the growing professional voice in the game, but typical of RWV to put pleasure and the public first.

But at least some of Robbie's campaign for brighter cricket to bring in the crowds was paying off at last. Following the popularity of the one-day International Cavaliers matches on Sundays, sponsored by Rothman's in the summer of 1966, the inauguration was announced of the Cricket World Cup in 1967, a triangular tournament of one-day matches between England, West Indies and the Rest of the World. The development and success of limited-overs cricket over the years shows how right he was, and although it would take nearly another forty years, the introduction and huge success of Twenty20 tournaments is the latest proof of his vision of the future for that form of cricket which always, weather permitting, produced a result. But his hopes for a more positive approach to first-class cricket were never fully realised. Setting an example with his creative declarations was generally viewed as merely another demonstration of his boundless over-confidence and not to be taken seriously. Reducing the number of overs allowed in each team's first innings found many supporters when half of all county cricket matches were failing to produce a result. Robbie believed 85 overs were more than enough and even proposed bringing this down to 65. Such restrictions were considered a step too far but, in response to falling over-rates which reduced the prospects for a result, the authorities were forced to demand that a minimum number of overs had to be bowled during each day. But that still did not guarantee a result which for Robbie was always the point of every game, at whatever level it was being played.

However, not everyone could see the benefits of 'brighter cricket'. Out of the blue, Robbie was shocked to receive a letter in 1967 from Ted Dexter accompanied by a copy of his new autobiography, *Dexter Declares*. In the letter he wrote:

> I am sending you a copy of my book before publication which I hope you enjoy reading as an entity. I do so because in my efforts to point out how severely English Cricket has been and still is affected by the whole 'brighter cricket' bogy, I find on re-reading, that I have been more personal about you in your time as chairman of selectors, than was perhaps necessary to make the point. I hope you can feel that, even if the point has been poorly or inadequately made, it is a genuine attempt to clear the game of 'brighter' cricket, so as to allow brighter cricketers, who need no encouraging, to flourish. I think I have accepted blame myself in full measure for those unsettled, though not wholly unsuccessful, times. I would love to have them over again.

In his attack on the campaign for brighter cricket, Dexter admitted that initially he was a supporter of Robbie's determination to bring crowds back into cricket grounds by ensuring that matches were played out by all players on both sides intending to achieve a result, win or lose, rather than avoid defeat: 'We both had dreams of what cricket could and should be and I was too young to know better.' He went on to suggest that Robbie had unrealistic expectations of commitment from players to play with enterprise from start to finish: 'There was a splendid dream going the rounds, the dream of a series of spell-binding cut-and-thrust games of cricket with everyone playing the game openly, hitting the ball gloriously and all the rest of it.'

Robbie's refused to be drawn into an exchange of views on the way cricket should be played and his reply to Dexter's letter was a masterpiece of restraint:

> At tuppence a page I think your book is good value for money, but after

your letter, I sent it round to my solicitor! You got the all clear today, so I am writing to thank you for all the compliments you pay me. Never mind, you gave me great pleasure over the six years you played Test cricket. I can assure you that despite your views of brighter cricket, nothing excites spectators more than seeing the batsman having a swing at the ball, hit or miss, and when in form you didn't often miss.

But there were more pleasant memories to enjoy and the opportunity to share some of them with others through the columns of *The Cricketer*. His first contribution appeared in the 1967 Spring Annual and was the one previously mentioned in 'Early Years in Stafford' and was entitled 'My First *Wisden*'. There was time for just one more article and, true to form, he couldn't resist the temptation to give some facts about his failures rather than his successes. In the June 1967 issue of *The Cricketer* he wrote 'On making a pair — or rather four!' where he listed the four matches in which he had the distinction of being dismissed first ball in each innings. Most cricketers would prefer to forget such ignominy and choose to write about their greatest achievements, but that wouldn't do for Robbie who loved stories against himself like his four 'king pairs' and always got a huge laugh out of telling them.

Kathleen wrote of Robbie's last year: 'He ate well and slept well, went to the office until within weeks of his death, mostly being driven there and back. He never complained, never once bemoaned his fate — just faded out.' He died at home on 12 December 1968 - they had now moved to an apartment not far from St John's Wood tube station — from bronchopneumonia, with Parkinson's Disease as a secondary factor. Three days later a tribute appeared in the *Sunday Telegraph* written by John Warr under the heading 'Never a dull moment with Walter around' in which he recalled that 'Walter Robins was the most stimulating and dynamic cricketer that I ever played with. Those may sound strong words but they will be echoed by his contemporaries at Highgate School, Cambridge University, Middlesex County Cricket Club and the England elevens of his time.' He added: 'He has enriched cricket with his skill, his humour and his liveliness.' The funeral took place at Golders Green Crematorium where David Sheppard took the service and made a short address. It was not possible to have an official memorial service at Lord's but this did not deter Kathleen from ensuring that 'Headquarters' would be his final resting place. At the first available opportunity she secretly placed Robbie's ashes in a shopping bag, cut off a corner and then unobtrusively walked around the playing perimeter of the ground, leaking them out as she went.

An obituary appeared in the 1969 Spring Annual of *The Cricketer* from his oldest and greatest friend, Ian Peebles, who wrote:

there departed from cricket its blithest spirit of a generation. He leaves behind him a blaze of achievements, rows, stories, incidents, affections and affronts. His not infrequent disasters, leavened by a wonderful and unfailing sense of humour, are amongst the warmest of the memories which remain so vividly with everyone who knew and played with him.

His obituary in the *Wisden* almanack of 1969 said that Robbie would 'live in history as one the most dynamic all-round cricketers of his time.' Among the tributes included was one from Doug Insole: 'Walter's death is a sad blow. He was the greatest exponent ever of "brighter cricket", though never for its own sake, but because he believed such cricket achieved greater success. As a selector his judgment of a player was excellent.'

Two years later in *Lord's: 1946-1970*, written by Ian Peebles in partnership with Diana Rait Kerr, Peebles took the opportunity to pay further tribute to Robbie: 'No cricketer ever brought to the game a more propitious mixture of devotion, enthusiasm, knowledge and humour. Nor did anyone ever strive harder to serve it in every sphere, not least by playing it as he believed it ought to be played — with joy and enterprise — on all occasions.'

That summer the President of Middlesex County Cricket Club, G.C.Newman, unveiled wooden benches in the Lord's gardens erected in memory of five Middlesex amateurs, A.J.Webb, F.T.Mann, N.E.Haig, G.E.V.Crutchley and R.W.V.Robins. Whenever members of the Robins family are able to gather together on match days they enjoy a picnic lunch sitting on the bench bearing Robbie's name, his sole memorial at the ground, and raise their glasses, rightly, in his memory.

Robbie's memorial bench in the garden behind the Warner Stand at Lord's.

Acknowledgements

This book could not have been written without co-operation and corroboration from Charles Robins and Richard Robins. Their response to my constant stream of questions while we exchanged more than 200 emails over a period of 18 months, together with the stories and anecdotes that flowed during a memorable lunch in the Committee dining room at Lord's last summer, enabled me to build a unique picture of their father and the impact his life had had on cricket, cricketers, and everyone around him.

I must also thank Guy Seaton of Stafford Cricket Club, who personally delivered to my home the club's committee minute books from 1888 to 1913; James Newton, the archivist at Highgate School, who provided access to *The Cholmeleian*, the monthly journal of Highgate School, covering the years from 1921 to 1925; Dr Jonathan Holme, Keeper of the Records at Queens' College, Cambridge; Neil Robinson at the MCC Library; Peter Wynne-Thomas, who supplied me with an index of all the significant references to Walter Robins in *The Cricketer* magazine as well as confirmation of his first-team appearances for Nottingham Forest Football Club; Philip Bailey and Gerald Hudd for their help on various statistical points, and David Jeater for his encouragement, patience, editorial skills and creative suggestions. Photographs in the book have come from a variety of sources and I am grateful to Patrick Jeater, Charles and Richard Robins, Roger Mann and David Taylor, in particular, for their assistance.

For their contributions to the production of the book, may I thank Richard Shaw and his colleagues at City Press Leeds Ltd and the Association's proofreaders for their good work.

Bromley, Kent
April 2013

Select Bibliography

(a) Books

H.S.Altham and E.W.Swanton, *A History of Cricket* (Third Edition),
  George Allen and Unwin, 1948
John Arlott, *Vintage Summer: 1947*, Eyre and Spottiswoode, 1967
Derek Birley, *A Social History of Cricket*, Aurum, 1999
Rob Cavallini, *Play Up Corinth: A History of the Corinthian Football Club*,
  Stadia, 2007
Colin Cowdrey, *M.C.C.: The Autobiography of a Cricketer*,
  Hodder and Stoughton, 1976
Ted Dexter, *Ted Dexter Declares*, Sportsman's Book Club, 1966
Bill Edrich, *Cricket Heritage*, Stanley Paul and Co, 1950
Alan Gibson, *The Cricket Captains of England*, Cassell, 1979
Benny Green, *The Lord's Companion*, Pavilion, 1981
Brian Heald, *Middlesex C.C.C. First-Class Records, 1850-1998*, Limlow Books,1999
Alan Hill, *Peter May: A Biography*, André Deutsch, 1996
Christopher Hilton: *Bradman and The Summer That Changed Cricket*,
  J.R.Books, 2009
David Lemmon, *The Official History of Middlesex County Cricket Club*,
  Guild Publishing, 1988
Tony Lewis, *Double Century: The Story of M.C.C. and Cricket*,
  Hodder and Stoughton, 1987
Christopher Martin-Jenkins, *The Complete Who's Who of Test Cricketers*, Orbis, 1980
Peter May, *A Game Enjoyed*, Stanley Paul and Co, 1985
Anthony Meredith, *Summers in Winter*, Kingswood, 1990
Andrew Murtagh, *A Remarkable Man*, Shire Publications, 2012
Ian Peebles, *Spinner's Yarn*, Collins, 1977
Tony Percival, *Staffordshire Cricketers 1872- 2002*, ACS Publications, 2003
Roland Perry, *The Don: The Definitive Biography of Sir Donald Bradman*,
  Frank Cass, 2000
Jack Pollard, *From Bradman to Border: Australian Cricket, 1948-1989*, Collins, 1990
Hon T.C.F.Prittie, *Mainly Middlesex*, Hutchison, 1946
Diana Rait Kerr and Ian Peebles, *Lord's 1946-1970*, George G.Harrap, 1971
Brian Rendell, *Gubby Under Pressure*, ACS Publications, 2007
Miranda Rijks, *The Eccentric Entrepreneur: Sir Julien Cahn*, The History Press, 2008
R.C.Robertson-Glasgow, *Cricket Prints*, T.Werner Laurie, 1943
Kathleen Robins, *RWV*, unpublished memoir, c 1970
Alan Ross, *Through the Caribbean: England in the West Indies 1960*,
  Hamish Hamilton, 1990
Mark Rowe, *The Victory Tests*, SportsBooks, 2010
E.W.Swanton, *Gubby Allen: Man of Cricket*, Hutchinson, 1985
E.W.Swanton, *West Indies Revisited: The M.C.C. Tour 1959-60*, Heinemann, 1960
E.W.Swanton, *Sort of a Cricket Person*, William Collins, 1972
David Sheppard, *Parson's Pitch*, Hodder and Stoughton, 1964
Allen Synge, *Sins of Omission: The Story of the Test Selectors 1899-1990*,
  Pelham Books, 1990
Fred Trueman, *Ball of Fire*, Mayflower, 1977
Fred Trueman, *The Thoughts of Trueman Now*, Macdonald and Jane's, 1979

Sir Pelham Warner, *The Book of Cricket* (Fourth Edition), Sporting Handbooks, 1945
Sir Pelham Warner, *Cricket Between Two Wars*, Chatto and Windus, 1942
Sir Pelham Warner, *Lord's 1787-1945*, George G.Harrap, 1946
Colin Weir, *The History of Cambridge University A.F.C. 1872-2003*, Yore, 2004
Marcus Williams (ed), *Double Century: 200 Years of Cricket in The Times*,
    Guild Publishing, 1985
Graeme Wright (ed), '*Wisden at Lord's: An Illustrated Anthology*,
    John Wisden and Co, 2005
Peter Wynne-Thomas, *Sir Julien Cahn's Team, 1923-1941*, ACS Publications, 1994

(b) Newspapers and Periodicals

The Cholmelian, Highgate School journal, various years
The Cricketer magazine, 1923 to 1969
The Times newspaper, 1923 to 1968
Wisden Cricketers' Almanack, 1913, 1923 to 1969

In addition to the above I have made good use of the database at
www.cricketarchive.com, and Australian newspaper material at trove.nla.gov.au.

Appendix
Career Statistics

Test Cricket: Batting and Fielding

Season	M	I	NO	R	HS	Ave	100	50	Ct
1929 South Africa	1	2	0	4	4	2.00	-	-	-
1930 Australia	2	4	2	70	50*	35.00	-	1	1
1931 New Zealand	1	1	0	12	12	12.00	-	-	-
1932 India	1	2	0	51	30	25.50	-	-	3
1933 West Indies	2	2	0	63	55	31.50	-	1	1
1935 South Africa	3	3	1	132	108	66.00	1	-	2
1936 India	2	2	0	76	76	38.00	-	1	2
1936/37 Australia	4	6	0	113	61	18.83	-	1	1
1937 New Zealand	3	5	1	91	38*	22.75	-	-	2
Totals	**19**	**27**	**4**	**612**	**108**	**26.60**	**1**	**4**	**12**

Test Cricket: Bowling

Season	O	M	R	W	BB	Ave	5i	10m
1929 South Africa	43	9	79	5	3-32	15.80	-	-
1930 Australia	85.2	7	338	10	4-51	33.80	-	-
1931 New Zealand	50	8	164	5	3-38	32.80	-	-
1932 India	31	9	96	3	2-39	32.00	-	-
1933 West Indies	63.4	5	220	11	6-32	20.00	1	-
1935 South Africa	87.0	16	264	9	3-73	29.33	-	-
1936 India	56.1	8	204	9	3-50	22.66	-	-
1936/37 Australia	56	3	220	4	2-31	55.00	-	-
1937 New Zealand	62.1	12	173	8	4-40	21.62	-	-
Totals (6-b)	**478.2**	**74)**						
(8-b)	**56**	**3)**	**1758**	**64**	**6-32**	**27.46**	**1**	**-**

Notes: Overs were of six balls throughout Robins' Test career, except in Australia in 1936/37 when they were of eight balls.

First-Class Cricket: Batting and Fielding

Season	M	I	NO	R	HS	Ave	100	50	Ct
1925	3	4	0	77	39	19.25	-	-	1
1926	15	22	2	284	37	14.20	-	-	12
1927	20	30	2	886	96	31.64	-	6	17
1928	28	47	3	1377	103	31.29	2	7	15
1929	34	48	5	1134	106	26.37	1	6	20
1929/30 (Argentina)	3	5	0	133	71	26.60	-	1	1
1930	11	16	3	397	140	30.53	1	2	9
1931	7	10	1	173	54	19.22	-	1	1
1932	7	7	0	170	46	24.28	-	-	7
1933	11	18	0	532	106	29.55	1	3	6
1934	14	24	2	685	65	31.13	-	6	5

1935	25	37	4	772	108	23.39	1	3	17
1936	24	34	3	863	77	27.83	-	6	13
1936/37 (Australia)	12	16	0	297	61	18.56	-	2	4
1937	29	42	5	1076	87	29.08	-	7	23
1938	28	41	3	989	137	26.02	1	4	11
1939	4	6	0	137	84	22.83	-	1	-
1945	3	5	0	58	33	11.60	-	-	2
1946	31	46	1	1397	129	31.04	3	6	8
1947	21	31	0	708	68	22.83	-	3	13
1948	17	22	0	735	101	33.40	1	3	10
1949	13	23	2	552	68	26.28	-	4	14
1950	11	17	1	308	58	19.25	-	1	6
1951 (Canada)	1	2	0	63	57	31.50	-	1	1
1951 (England)	2	4	0	16	16	4.00	-	-	-
1952	3	5	1	62	25	15.50	-	-	-
1954	1	2	1	1	1*	1.00	-	-	1
1958 (Ireland)	1	1	0	2	2	2.00	-	-	-
Totals	**379**	**565**	**39**	**13884**	**140**	**26.39**	**11**	**73**	**217**

Notes: Robins was dismissed 238 times caught (45%); 205 times bowled (39%); 37 times stumped (7%, an unusually high proportion); 26 times lbw (5%); 18 times run out (4%) and twice hit wicket. He was dismissed most often by T.W.J.Goddard, fifteen times, and by A.R.Gover, T.F.Smailes and A.P.Freeman eight times. He played 258 matches for Middlesex, scoring 9,337 runs at 26.37 and taking 137 catches.

First-Class Cricket: Bowling

Season	O	M	R	W	BB	Ave	5i	10m
1926	10	4	13	2	2-7	6.50	-	-
1927	112	17	440	6	2-4	73.33	-	-
1928	761.5	101	2654	90	6-61	29.48	3	-
1929	1154.4	156	3489	162	8-69	21.53	9	1
1929/30 (Argentina)	119.4	24	335	28	6-40	11.96	3	2
1930	383.1	51	1195	53	6-73	22.54	5	-
1931	204	26	616	24	5-26	25.66	1	-
1932	215.1	33	585	32	6-45	18.28	3	-
1933	311.1	39	947	36	7-36	26.30	3	-
1934	411.4	53	1244	42	5-39	29.61	2	-
1935	503.3	86	1456	80	6-39	18.20	7	-
1936	533.1	107	1553	82	8-105	18.93	5	-
1936/37 (Australia)	154.3	8	638	16	4-63	39.87	-	-
1937	662.2	97	1980	99	6-40	20.00	5	-
1938	470.3	66	1705	68	7-77	25.07	3	-
1939	55.7	4	221	11	6-86	20.09	1	-
1945	58.3	2	250	8	4-70	31.25	-	-
1946	373.4	42	1171	48	7-71	24.39	4	1
1947	224.1	39	687	26	4-37	26.42	-	-
1948	117	17	395	13	3-50	30.38	-	-
1949	109	15	391	14	3-36	27.92	-	-
1950	61.4	11	252	13	4-17	19.38	-	-
1951 (Canada)	29.2	2	75	5	3-62	15.00	-	-
1951 (England)	31	3	86	2	1-25	43.00	-	-
1952	46	6	157	4	2-40	39.25	-	-
1954	15	6	38	4	4-27	9.50	-	-
1958 (Ireland)	3	0	7	1	1-7	7.00	-	-

Totals (6-b)	6921.1 1003)						
(8-b)	210.2	12) 22580	969	8-69	23.30	54	4

Note: Overs were of six balls throughout Robins' first-class career, except in Australia in 1936/37 and in England in 1939 when they were of eight balls. He took his wickets at the rate of one per 44.59 balls and conceded runs at a rate equivalent to 3.13 runs per six-ball over. Of his 969 wickets, 395 (41%) were caught; 249 (26%) were bowled; 173 (18%) were lbw; 143 (15%, an unusually high proportion) were stumped and nine (1%) were hit wicket. He took 32 catches off his own bowling. He dismissed five batsmen eight times or more; these were A.P.Freeman and H.S.Squires, nine times; F.S.Lee, A.F.Wensley H.W.Parks, eight times. For Middlesex he took 669 wickets at 22.28, including 40 five-wicket returns.

First-Class Cricket: Centuries (11)

Score	For	Opponent	Venue	Season
103	Cambridge Univ[1]	MCC	Lord's	1928
101*	Cambridge Univ[2]	Oxford Univ	Lord's	1928
106	Middlesex[1]	Somerset	Taunton	1929
140	Middlesex[2]	Cambridge Univ	Fenner's	1930
106	MCC[1]	Kent	Lord's	1933
108	England[1]	South Africa	Old Trafford	1935
137	Middlesex[1]	Sussex	Lord's	1938
129	Middlesex[1]	Nottinghamshire	Trent Bridge	1946
102	Middlesex[1]	Essex	Lord's	1946
116	MCC[1]	Yorkshire	Scarborough	1946
101	Middlesex[1]	Kent	Dover	1948

Notes: The index figures [1] and [2] in this and the following table indicate the innings in which the feat was achieved.

First-Class Cricket: Six wickets or more in an innings (25)

Analysis	For	Opponent	Venue	Season
21.4-0-61-6	Cambridge Univ	MCC[2]	Lord's	1928
43-6-126-6	Middlesex	Warwickshire[1]	Lord's	1928
15.4-5-29-6	Middlesex	Leicestershire[1]	Lord's	1929
32-6-69-8	Middlesex	Gloucestershire[2]	Lord's	1929
19.1-2-53-6	Middlesex	Nottinghamshire[2]	Lord's	1929
38-7-129-6	Middlesex	Leicestershire[1]	Leicester (AR)	1929
17.1-5-43-6	Middlesex	Somerset[2]	Taunton	1929
27.3-3-89-6	The Rest	Nottinghamshire[2]	The Oval	1929
20.3-5-40-6	Sir Julien Cahn's XI	Argentina[1]	Buenos Aires	1929/30
25-2-65-6	Sir Julien Cahn's XI	Argentina[2]	Buenos Aires	1929/30
25.1-0-73-6	Middlesex	Derbyshire[1]	Lord's	1930
40-8-101-6	Middlesex	Somerset[1]	Lord's	1930
17.2-1-45-6	Middlesex	Worcestershire[2]	Lord's	1932
20.5-2-45-6	Middlesex	Kent[1]	Lord's	1932
18.2-4-36-7	Middlesex	Hampshire[2]	Lord's	1933
11.5-1-32-6	England	West Indies[1]	Lord's	1933
20-2-58-6	Middlesex	Warwickshire[1]	Lord's	1935
16-4-39-6	Middlesex	Essex[2]	Lord's	1935
35-8-107-6	Middlesex	Nottinghamshire[1]	Trent Bridge	1935
33.4-4-105-8	England XI	Indians[1]	Folkestone	1936
26.4-8-40-6	Middlesex	Lancashire[1]	Old Trafford	1937
17.4-3-69-6	Middlesex	Sussex[1]	Lord's	1938

18.2-3-77-7	Middlesex	Hampshire[2]	Lord's	1938
18.7-0-86-6	Middlesex	Surrey[1]	The Oval	1939
27.3-4-71-7	Middlesex	Cambridge Univ[1]	Fenner's	1946

Notes: Overs were of six balls in all these instances except the 1939 match. At Buenos Aires in 1929/30, the first match was at the Belgrano club ground and the second at the Hurlingham club.

R.V.C.Robins

Walter's son Charles played in 60 first-class matches in England between 1953 and 1962, mostly for Middlesex and MCC. A right-hand lower-order batsman, he scored 1,055 runs at 12.71, took 107 wickets at 33.61 as a leg-break and googly bowler, and held 19 catches. His best bowling return was seven for 78 for Middlesex against Cambridge University at Fenner's in 1954.

Sources: www.cricketarchive.com, Wisden Cricketers'Almanack

Index

A page number in brackets indicates an illustration.